Efficacy of English Teacher Development Programmes in Government Social Welfare Residential Schools in Andhra Pradesh and Telangana

Efficacy of English Teacher Development Programmes in Government Social Welfare Residential Schools in Andhra Pradesh and Telangana

Godavarthi Govindaiah

GYAN

Published by

Gyan Publishing House
5, Ansari Road
Daryaganj, New Delhi-110002
Phone: 011-47034999, 9811692060
E-mail: books@gyanbooks.com

Distribution Network
gyanbooks.com
India, USA, Canada, UK, Australia, France

ISBN: 978-93-6920-738-1 (PB)
First Published, 2025

Printed at: Gyan Press, Delhi.

Efficacy of English Teacher Development Programmes in Government Social Welfare Residential School in Andhra Pradesh and Telangana
Author: Godavarthi Govindaiah

Dedicated to my Beloved Father

Shri Godavarthi Balaiah

Contents

Foreword

Andhra Pradesh, as we know, took the lead way back in 1971 to provide quality education to SC children from rural areas through the residential schools. Later in 1983-84, the Government of AP started nearly 46 schools under the management of the Department of Social Welfare funded by the World Bank. Much later in 1987, the *Social Welfare Residential Educational Institutes Society* (SWREIS) was established with the main focus on establishing and maintaining the schools. They provide quality secondary, technical, vocational education, balanced nutrition, medical care as well as organise co-curricular activities through these schools to underprivileged sections of the society.

Classes are generally organised from Grade V to XII through Telugu medium.The students are highly motivated but their competence in English is poor. This study states that "...this can be attributed, to some extent, to the fact that regional-medium learners start learning English when they are around 8 years of age i.e. when they are in class III.... and English, unfortunately, is often taught through the mother tongue". In the new education policy, it is envisaged that the use of mother tongue at lower levels would help children acquire other languages at higher levels. In the light of this it would be interesting to see what kind of perceptions the teachers hold.

Most teachers working for AP and Telangana SWREIS are trained teachers. The student-teacher ratio is also very good at 1:19. This book focuses on the experiences of English language teachers of both AP and Telangana working in SWREIS. An attempt has been made to understand the language teaching methods being used in AP and Telangana SWREIS, in order to identify and suggest practical ways by which the teaching of a second language can be facilitated in underprivileged regional medium, and English medium contexts. The book also tries to showcase the impact of various training programmes have had on the classroom practices of these teacher.

If the Governments of AP and Telangana consider implementing some of the suggestions outlined in this book titled "*Efficacy of English Teacher Development Programmes in Social Welfare Residential Schools in Andhra Pradesh and Telangana*", it would be a step in the right direction.

Prof. Surabhi Bharati

The English and Foreign Languages University, Hyderabad

Preface

Teacher development programmes stand as pillars in education, shaping the quality and character of teacher education across various landscapes. These programmes, designed to refine, enhance, and augment educators' existing knowledge, ultimately determine the calibre of teachers emerging from such initiatives. Attempt has been made to unfold within this intricate web of professional development, delving into the effectiveness of teacher development programmes in the context of secondary school English educators in the Social Welfare Residential Schools of Andhra Pradesh and Telangana States.

As the curtains rise, the narrative pivots around the profound impact of these programmes on teachers' pedagogical prowess, the essence of their classroom dynamics, and the resultant learning outcomes of their students. In a pioneering move, Andhra Pradesh took strides by establishing residential schools at the secondary education level for the underprivileged in 1971, setting the stage for a transformative educational journey. The Andhra Pradesh Social Welfare Residential Educational Institutes Society (APSWREIS) emerged as a beacon of hope, championing the cause of quality education for disadvantaged communities, weaving together a tapestry of academic excellence, co-curricular vibrancy, and holistic student support.

Amidst this backdrop, this book navigates through the corridors of APSWREIS, shedding light on the triumphs and tribulations encountered by educators and learners alike. As the narrative unfolds, it becomes evident that while the students exhibit unwavering enthusiasm, particularly towards the English language, their journey is fraught with linguistic challenges. The pedagogical landscape, heavily influenced by regional-medium instruction, grapples with the problem of language acquisition, compounded by limited exposure and conducive environments for English language practice. At the helm of this transformative journey stand the educators, tasked with sculpting young minds amidst myriad constraints. This book unveils their multifaceted role, juxtaposed against the backdrop of teacher development initiatives, seeking to unravel the symbiotic relationship between professional growth and classroom practice. Further examines the confluence of teacher training methodologies, teaching approaches, and the evolving landscape of teacher autonomy, offering glimpses into the transformative potential of teacher development programmes.

This book traverses uncharted territories, charting a course towards pedagogical enlightenment and professional growth. Anchored in empirical inquiry, the study endeavours to bridge the chasm between theory and practice, offering pragmatic insights and actionable recommendations for the educational fraternity. As this book unfolds, it invites stakeholders to embark on a transformative educational odyssey marked by resilience, introspection, and a shared commitment to academic excellence. I have attempted to bring forth together the threads of empirical inquiry, theoretical underpinnings, and practical insights. As we embark on this voyage of research, let us collectively endeavour to illuminate the path towards a brighter, more inclusive educational landscape.

Godavarthi Govindaiah
Department of English
School of Languages, Linguistics & Indology
Maulana Azad National Urdu University, Hyderabad

# Acknowledgement

I would like to express my heartfelt gratitude to the Almighty God for helping me in completion of this book. I am deeply indebted to Professor Pingali Sailaja, for her unwavering encouragement, guidance, and support. Without her kindness and assistance, this book would not have been possible.

I extend my thanks to the teachers, principals, APSWREIS Secretary, Deputy Director, and Academic Coordinator who generously participated in my research. My sincere appreciation goes to the APSWREIS College and School Principal, Vice-Principal, teachers, and students for their cooperation and warm hospitality during my observation of their classes.

I am especially grateful to the English teachers and resource persons whose insights were invaluable for this book. I also extend my thanks to everyone else who contributed, big or small.

I am truly grateful to Dr D. Vishwa Prasad, Dr Ravi Prakash, and Dr Viswanth for their meticulous proofreading and valuable suggestions.

My heartfelt thanks to my beloved wife, Vijaya, for her unwavering support and understanding have been invaluable throughout this journey.

Finally, I want to express my gratitude to my wonderful children, Joy Kaspar and Ben Danish, for their enthusiastic support throughout the writing of this book.

Godavarthi Govindaiah

Department of English

School of Languages, Linguistics & Indology

Maulana Azad National Urdu University, Hyderabad

Chapter - 1

Secondary School Teacher Development Programmes

The State Government of Andhra Pradesh has established the residential schools at secondary education level for poorer sections of the society in 1971. To provide quality education to young talented Scheduled Caste (SC) children coming from rural areas, the State Government of Andhra Pradesh has started 46 residential schools for Scheduled Caste children during 1983-84 under the management of the Department of Social Welfare funded by World Bank. Andhra Pradesh Social Welfare Residential Educational Institutions Society (APSWREIS) is the State level organisation for the management of these schools, came into existence in 1987. The main activities of the APSWREIS are to establish and maintain Social Welfare Residential schools and colleges. APSWREI Society aims to provide quality secondary education, technical and vocational education. Co-curricular activities, balanced nutrition and medical care are provided through these schools to the underprivileged sections of the society.

The secondary school English teacher development programmes is one of the teacher development programmes (TDP) has been implemented in Andhra Pradesh and Telangana States. We have examined the efficacy of teacher development programmes in Andhra Pradesh Social Welfare Residential Educational Institutions Society (APSWREIS). It is based on the programmes that the teachers attended, the objectives of the programmes, the opinions of the teachers, and resource persons and the researcher's classroom observation of regular classroom teaching of the teachers. The classrooms in these schools are spacious enough to seat 35 to 40 students per class. They are well-ventilated and provided equipped with basic infrastructural facilities. Students are quiet, well-disciplined, and regular in attending classes. The schools have wonderful infrastructure facilities by way of well-equipped libraries, computer labs, and TV lounges. Extra-curricular activities such as indoor and outdoor games and National Cadet Corps (NCC) are also encouraged and made available. These facilities however, are available only in Hyderabad, Secunderabad, and Ranga Reddy districts and not in all schools.

The students are highly motivated to learn something every day, especially in English. Ironically, they do well in all other subjects except English. This can be attributed, to some extent, to the fact that regional-medium learners start learning English when they are around 8 years i.e. when they are in class III. By this time, they have already achieved basic linguistic competence in their mother tongue. And, the English that is learnt in class is not practised because they do not have enough exposure. English, unfortunately, is often taught through the mother tongue and whatever little English learners hear is only from the teacher. These schools have classes from VI-X and Junior colleges. The teachers teach students in Telugu, and English is also taught through the mother tongue. As the students are drawn from economically backward sections, the facilities they enjoy and the support they get from home is minimal. Therefore, most students struggle to cope with the language and the subjects in school. The teachers do not have a high opinion of their abilities and this is reflected in their attitudes and teaching. The students are taught English through the extensive use of the mother tongue. No attempt is made to use the target language in the classroom and any such suggestions do not evoke a positive or enthusiastic response. Thus, the target language use is kept to a minimum and the mother tongue is used for all activities in the classroom.

Like all regional medium learners, unlike their English medium counterparts, students of APSWREIS get to study English only when they come to class III. Their early years are spent gaining proficiency in the mother tongue. The students do not get an opportunity to practise communication skills in or outside the classroom. The teachers do not seem keen to help them cultivate basic skills in using the target language. Maybe teachers are not properly trained or equipped with requirements of the students' needs. "Guides" are used to dictate answers or put them up on the board for the examination point of view, and therefore all language-learning stops with "questions and answers," in their notebooks. Learners are poor at spelling, vocabulary, reading, and grammar, in short, all aspects of language. It was also noticed in the study mentioned above, that the students were willing to learn provided they had a source to rely on and help them out in times of difficulty.

The present book focuses on the experiences of English language teachers of APSWREIS. An attempt has been made to look at, briefly, the teacher training, education and development and the nature and types of training carried out in the APSWREIS. Furthermore, the study tries to indicate areas that require due attention in English Language Teacher Training Programmes offered to the teachers working at APSWREIS. An investigation has been undertaken in the context of teachers who have been teaching under APSWREIS, where the medium of instruction is supposed to be English. Though most of the learners have studied English as a second language, their exposure to the language is found to be very limited. In most of the classrooms, it is the teacher who is found speaking the English language and the learners acting as passive listeners.

As mentioned earlier, the teacher's communicative and linguistic competence in English is meagre. The teacher, often, is not equipped to understand the learners' problems, and meet the academic needs of the learners. However, to meet the learners' needs in APSWREIS, the teachers are found making use of collaborative teaching techniques, and adhering to novel learning / teaching strategies. It is worthwhile to examine the teaching/learning strategies that the teachers are required to adhere to, and innovative methodologies to fulfill the learners' needs.

We have explored teachers' teaching strategies, teacher/learner's strategies and the training programmes. A study of these strategies will indicate whether the teachers are moving towards autonomous teaching and learning strategies in coping with the teaching situation. We have attempted is to gain an understanding of language teaching, the process of teaching strategies for teachers with special focus on the role of teacher development. This study focuses on Andhra Pradesh Social Welfare Residential Educational Institutes Society (APSWREIS) in-service teachers. The study presumes that the teachers should have adequate information about effective teaching strategies/learning strategies through English language teaching methodology. Teacher cultural attitudes and beliefs are also important for the development of specific-school students like those in APSWRIES.

Teachers are qualified but not competent enough to understand the learning problems of the students in the classroom. The teachers' job entails giving inputs and feedback both in the classroom and after class hours. They are responsible for time management, round-the-clock observation of the students and maintaining study hours. However, these responsibilities are either not undertaken by the teachers, or they do not wish to be burdened with additional charge after class hours. Teachers have 30-35 students in each section of the class. Most of the teachers are qualified with TGT-PGT (Graduate Trained Teacher- Post Graduate trained Teacher). Some have PGDTE (Post Graduate Diploma in Teaching of English) from CIEFL, Hyderabad. The Teacher-pupil ratio in the APSWREIS schools is 1:19, whereas it is 1:37 in Government secondary schools. Lower teacher pupil ratio is conducive for improving the performance. Not only does teacher-pupil ratio decide the quality, but also the availability of teachers to handle different subjects. The research traces out some of the important aspects of teacher development programmes. These schools were established 35 years ago. There is no research in the field of ELT focusing on APSWREIS schools.

We have attempted to suggest practical ways by which the teaching of a second language can be facilitated in general, and specifically, in a regional, English medium and underprivileged context has been made. When learners do not have much exposure to the second language in their environment, it may be useful to help learners approach the second language from a holistic perspective. Exposing learners to English language in natural contexts could do this. Based on the positive response received from students in a research study undertaken with the objectives mentioned above (Govindaiah, 2004), a few activities that enable effective learning in the classroom are outlined here.

The research study mentioned above was done at the APSWREIS Schools. APSWREIS schools are residential schools run by the state government for the benefit of the children of the poor and the under-privileged. There are four reasons why teacher development is required. Teachers are a source of language; they serve as learning support, thus giving motivation and stimulation for learning and serve as a point of reference. Keeping this in mind, one of the primary objects of any teacher development programme is then to give the teachers an opportunity to gain exposure to planning, implementation and evaluation of specific content areas in relation to the classroom. This is best done through understanding how methodology is translated in the classroom through the use of appropriate material. In spite of all the development programmes the teachers and schools experience the problems of inadequate training or orientation of teachers on the materials; shortage of competent teachers; lack of facilities of library, laboratory, equipment and teaching aids; late arrival of text books and supplementary materials; weak linkage between the community and teacher (school); parents often not invited to school; lack of suitable classrooms for teaching; the concept of integrated approach not clearly understood by teachers.

These problems were stated by the teachers themselves at the teacher enrichment programme at CIEFL, Hyderabad on 12th March 2007 that I participated in. However, not all the problems are applicable to all the teachers. What steps have been taken to incorporate teacher development strategies into APSWREIS schools, and how successful have these efforts of teacher development programmes in these special schools? The purpose of this book is to consider how teacher development strategies are treated in one area of endeavour in the field of ELT; namely, Teacher Development programmes. The goal is to determine to what extent, if any, current TDP (teacher development programmes) contribute to the development of teachers' skills use of teacher development strategies. Which strategies are useful for TD in evidence in current TDP? Training programmes for teachers, Refresher courses for English teachers of APSWREIS are regularly conducted by APSWREIS and other organisations such as, CIEFL (EFLU), Hyderabad, SCERT and so on. Unfortunately, some of the teachers are not intimated in time. Moreover, the teachers feel that a one-week programme is not sufficient. They need more training on methodology and introducing the skills to the learners from the students' point of view. These training sessions are conducted at the time of the students' final examination. Out of 296 institutions, in 199 institutions Computer Labs are provided to keep up the students' abilities in computer knowledge and in the remaining 97 institutions, one computer along with printer is available. Mana TV a special channel meant for education. Out of 296 schools, in 194 Schools KU Band facilities are provided for distance education, regularly telecast for the benefit of the students, and in the remaining 102 institutions it is in the process of being provided.

The teacher has a greater impact on students than any other factor in the school system. The methods that the teacher adopts for him/her to develop his/her professional development are therefore very important. The main objectives of teacher development should be to (i) produce teachers who are academically qualified, professionally skilled, attitudinally and ethically committed and dedicated to their teaching, (ii) prepare teachers who can confidently promote active learning and the development of problem solving skills through a learner-centered approach using a curriculum where content and methods are integrated, (iii) establish a system and culture of continuous teacher development programme from in-service education and training using diverse modes of delivery, (iv) equip teachers with knowledge of their students' physical, social, emotional and intellectual development including those with special needs so that they will be able to plan appropriate lessons, (v) develop communication skills and instructional leadership qualities necessary for facilitating co-curricular activities and community involvement, (vi) equip teachers with knowledge and ability in classroom management, which fosters constructive student inquiries and interaction, (vii) prepare teachers who can effectively apply continuous assessment and evaluation to student's learning and have basic knowledge and application of action research, and (viii) employ teacher educators, especially English Language teacher educators, who have appropriate knowledge in English teacher development; actively encourage student teacher to develop their learning potential. Finally, we have suggested remedies to offset the drawbacks.

Chapter - 2

Teacher Education, Training and Development

We have discussed issues in teacher training and education and teacher development programmes in Telangana and Andhra Pradesh. We have tried to present concepts and practices of teacher education discussed by researchers. First, a historical overview of teacher education, models of teacher education and approaches to second language teaching, and second language teacher training, education and teacher development programmes in India are discussed. This chapter in particular concentrates on the practices of teacher development programmes offered to the teachers working at APSWREIS in Andhra Pradesh and Telangana regions.

The aspect of Teacher development has a potentially significant role to play in effective teaching/learning strategies of English teachers. The notion of teacher development has its roots in the evolution of perceptions of teacher preparation. Teacher development can be seen as an intended form of teacher training and teacher education. These three terms along with terms like 'professional development', 'self-development', and 'faculty development' are sometimes used to mean the same thing: teacher preparation.

2.1. Language Teacher Education

The history of language teacher education is a chequered one; the first teacher trailing course started in London in 1962. These courses were to lead later to certificate level courses such as TESOL CELTA, DELTA, etc. Renewed interest in the 1980's was the result of the work of Council of Europe. Speaking about the advances in teacher education, Richards and Nunan had this to offer! The field of Language teacher education is a relatively underexplored one in both second and foreign language teaching. The literature on teacher education in language teaching is slight compared with the literature on issues such as methods and techniques for classroom teaching. Few of the articles published in the last twenty years are data-based and most consist of anecdotal wish lists of what is best for the teacher. (Richards and Nunan, 1990: xi)

Crandall (2000; as cited in Borg, 2012, p. 216) had this to say of literature dealing with teacher education. The LTE courses signified the following:

(i) A shift from transmission, product-oriented the theories to constructivist, process-oriented theories of learning, teaching and teacher-learning.

(ii) Efforts initiated to transform teaching through a focus on situated teacher cognition and practice and the development of concrete, relevant linkages between theory and practice throughout the teacher education programme.

(iii) A growing recognition that teacher's prior learning experiences play a powerful role in shaping their views of effective teaching and learning and their teaching practices.

(iv) A growing concern that teaching be viewed as a profession (similar to medicine or law) with respect for the role of teachers in developing theory and directing their own professional development through collaborative observation, teacher research and inquiry, and sustained in-service programmes.

Where language teacher education is concerned, (Borg, 2011) identifies six major themes including the following:

Teacher cognition: This exercises a vital role on teaching because it is concerned with teacher knowledge, experience, and beliefs. These in turn determine what teachers do in an ESL classroom and why they do it.

(a) Teacher cognition views teachers' active, thinking and decision-makers whose action are influenced by affective and psychological dimensions in teaching.

(b) Knowledge base for LTE; broadly speaking, teachers need to have adequate command of the language they are teaching and knowledge of what and how to teach. Thus, according to Richards (1988), teaching, teaching skills, communication skills, subject matter knowledge, pedagogical reasoning and contextual knowledge are essential for any teacher. The development of an integrated knowledge base that any teacher can use is of the essence for any teacher development programmed to achieve its objective.

(c) Knowledge about language; teacher is required to know the rules of grammar and usage about the language they intend to teach; this would in turn help teacher to design activities using authentic materials and take learning a new levels of imagination.

(d) Reflective practice; Dewey (1933), Schon (1983) and Wallace (1991) were pioneers in the field.

(e) Teachers are expected to introspect and look objectively at their own teaching practices and beliefs in order to become aware of such practices and improve on them. Action research, journal writing, teacher study groups, teacher get together, can all lead to positive teacher reflection on and discussion of their own teaching practices. Such reflection should necessarily be voluntary and not governed by motives of compulsion or indifference. Again, very few studies have been able to prove that there is a direct and positive relationship between teacher reflection and improved language teaching and learning. All that studies on reflective practice definitely leads to a positive impact on teacher attitudes and beliefs.

(f) Practicum: This refers to duration of practice teaching in real classrooms, an important component in LTE classrooms. Potential teachers are observed by teachers who have been in the field for long and such teachers provide feedback to teacher candidates on their performance. The primary goal of practicum is to provide teachers in the making with training in how to teach effectively and develop their skills as teachers. Practicum also helps teachers' use pedagogical reasoning as a tool in the language classroom.

(g) There are, however, several unanswered questions and loose ends; the practicum is not a fool proof method to judge everything about a teacher nor can the exercise be said to benefit every teacher candidate. The exact nature of the "triadic relationship involving student teachers, university supervisors and school-based mentors, and how this relationship shapes teacher learning on the practicum are also issues we know little about." (Borg, 2011, p. 221).

Teacher research: This refers to research embarked on by teachers to investigate "aspects of their own professional practices with a view to enhancing, first, their understanding of these and, subsequently, the quality of their work." (Borg, 2011, p. 221)

Teacher research goes beyond a very reductionist assumption about teachers starting to research certain basic questions based on their experience in the classroom. Teacher research is intrinsically tied with the larger issues of social, emotional, psychological, institutional, economic and political considerations. In order to comprehend Language Teacher Education fully, much importance needs to be accorded to the factors mentioned above, and overlooking some or any of these factors would defeat the very purpose of research.

Teacher research as a body of knowledge varies from country to country and from state to state. To fully comprehend and appreciate teacher research demands a lot of homework on the part of teachers, mentors, teacher trainers and teacher educators.

(i) In addition to the six primary factors, Borg identifies other related factors that impact language teacher education. These are:

(ii) Teacher educator development: this deals with such issues as the background of teacher educators, their skills and expertise, the skills and knowledge they would need additionally, and their interest in continuing to be language teacher educators.

(iii) Novice teachers: this is an important issue since student teachers transition from novices to real time teachers. It becomes equally important to ask how many teachers continue in the profession and how many find language teacher education useful for professional development.

Teacher expertise: This concerns the background knowledge and expertise that teacher come equipped with and the knowledge they would need in future. Teacher expertise will determine how efficient and successful teacher training programmes are and how they nurture novice teachers into professionals.

Though teacher education is an integral and indispensable part of teaching-learning process, not enough research has been initiated to throw light on the relationships between teacher education and student learning. While some studies hold that arriving at a relationship between teacher education and student learning is hard, the final or even a very conclusive answer is not easy in coming.

2.2. Teacher Training

The concept of training arises from a behaviourist notion of teaching/ learning. The process of teaching and learning is seen as an outcome of set patterns of behaviour. Training may be narrowly conceived in behaviourist terms with a sense of a teacher as a passive recipient being modified by systematic treatment or being dragged along by the power of some other force than the teacher's own. (Sawyer and Jones 1985:12).

The concept of Training, it has been pointed out, 'is like telling: Do this in this way' (McGrath, 1986:3). The term, training, evokes the notion of drill or practice. A trained person is said to be one who performs a task or a set of tasks in an accepted manner. The set of Teacher Training Programmers are often seen as being limited to the teaching of instructional methods, classroom management strategies, and the teacher – in most cases is expected to learn to use established techniques and conform to pre-determined types of behaviour. This view is highly criticized for the fact that it leaves very little freedom for the teacher.

2.3. Teacher Development

The notion of teacher development suggests that teachers have freedom to create new tasks for the learners, to do tasks in the classroom. Teachers are teaching and learning something in the classroom, which is not static or rigid; teachers should be flexible, and autonomy is desirable. It gives space for the teacher to adopt and respond to different situations in different ways. The aspect of teacher development recognizes the teacher's ability to create appropriate ways of realising instructional objectives. Here it is important to note that teacher development does not undermine the value of teacher 'training' and teacher education. Rather, it uses them for nurturing the growth of a teacher. The inter-relationships among these three aspects of teacher preparation can be summed up as follows.

> ...teacher training courses (programme) focus on practical skills, teacher education includes those, but extends the focus to professional awareness and an expansion of professional and interpersonal knowledge and teacher development includes all of the previous two, and broadens the concept out to include more personal and interpersonal as well as professional aspects and values. In share the difference in emphasis which justify the use of all these three terms in that while training focuses on doing and education focuses on knowing development focuses on being. (O' Brien, 1986:30).

'Teacher development' incorporates teacher training as well as teacher education. It can be viewed from two different perspectives. In the system-centered view of professional development where the requirements of the educational system are considered supreme, the purposes of training programmes are to correct teacher deficiencies in the necessary knowledge and skills. But the individual centered view of teacher development puts the focus on the self-perceived needs of the individual teacher. The assumption is that teachers are persons first and as individuals their professional development needs enhancement.

There is a progressive consensus on an approach to teacher preparation in ELT domain for its major shift from the notions 'teacher training' or 'teacher education' to 'teacher development' (Richards and Nunan, 1990; Swan, 1993). The component 'Teacher training' is understood as a behaviourist notion which involves drilling of set patterns and behaviour (Sayer and Jones, 1985:20). The teacher is a passive recipient of systematic treatment from trainer. Teacher has no freedom but he/she is expected to only absorb pre-defined and pre-determined methods and techniques from the trainer. On the other hand, in a teacher education programme, the teacher will be given freedom to make informed choices and objectives to generate his or her professional skills. It is like "developing the teacher's individual skills so that he or she can adapt to and function in any situation" (Larsen-Freeman, 1983:265).

On the other hand, this approach does not give sufficient focus to influencing factors like teacher experience, teacher personality, teacher attitude and his/her socio-cultural conditions. Though teacher-education programmes involve the teacher to some extent, the teacher trainer considerably dominates the teacher. Many academicians and experts of research in the field believe that teacher development offers ample of space to adapt and respond to different contexts in varied ways. Larsen-Freeman says,

> "development... focuses on the individual teacher: on the process of reflection, examination and change which can lead him or her to do a better job and to their personal and professional growth" (Freeman, 1982: 21-22).

Teacher development programmes not only synthesize with the contents of teacher training and teacher education programmes but also focus on teachers' experience, attitude and socio-cultural conditions. Their internal relationship is clearly stated by O'Brien as follows:

> Teacher training focuses on practical skills, teacher education includes those, but extends the focus to professional awareness and the expansion of professional and interpersonal knowledge and the teacher development programme includes the previous two and broadens the concept out, to include more personal and interpersonal as well as professional aspects and values. In short, the differences in emphasis is that while training focuses on doing, education focuses on knowing, and development focuses on being (O' Brien, 1986: 30).

Teacher development may be said not to be fixed to a particular time but goes on throughout service. The teacher accommodates himself/herself to reflect on his/her class room teaching in order to find out his/her own mistakes and propose suitable solutions to the problems. Thus, teacher development programmes encourage trainees to learn through self-reflection, identify and fix the problems and grow professionally. It may be noted that the aspect of Teacher development can be shaped through two stages: one is pre-service and the other being in-service programmes. Schubert (1986) mentions that pre-service programmes are the beginning of a 'professional journey' for a teacher. The programme consists of three features, viz., General Educational Courses, Professional Education Courses, and Student teaching and other clinical approaches. The objective of these courses is to improve the teacher's ability 'to adjust more fully to new and different situations' and to build a strong foundation for the beginning of real teaching and a real teaching-learning situation (Schubert, 1985: 382-385). In-service programmes are the real initiators of teacher development. It is an ongoing process of interaction between various factors, experiences and influences that run throughout their tenure of service. Teacher development will be influenced by teacher's participation in teacher development programmes like orientation workshops, refresher courses, research-based development projects etc, and other factors like teacher's commitment, his/her sensitivity to the current education system and policies of government and his/her desire to be dynamic and resourceful in the classroom.

2.3. Teacher Education: National Policy on Education (NPE)

Perhaps the earliest document that formally laid down broad educational policies for the country was the one published by Central Advisory Board of Education in 1952. Headed by Dr Lakshmanaswami Mudaliar, Vice Chancellor, Madras University, the commission submitted a blueprint outlining the educational policies for India. Following this, in 1967 Parliament constituted a committee to draft a National Policy on Education. One of the important observations of NPE was to put in place a uniform educational structure across the length and breadth of the country. Accordingly, in November 1974, the Central Advisory Board of Education adopted a resolution that recommended having 10+2+3 system of education all over India. NCERT (National Council of Educational Research and Training) framed a curriculum to reflect the then educational needs of students, syllabus, textbooks, and evaluation patterns were all determined by NCERT. This pattern was adopted by many states and the Central Board of Secondary Education (CBSE) was invested with the huge responsibility of looking after the needs of several thousand students pursuing education in central schools in India. Controversy broke out soon after over the syllabus and textbooks prepared by NCERT for students of IX and X Standard as the textbooks were perceived to be too many, too voluminous and completely indifferent to the skill sets necessary for the job market.

There was a committee constituted under the stewardship of Dr Malcolm Adiseshaiah an eminent economist and V.C; University of Madras to revisit the curriculum of plus two stage of school education, with an emphasis on vocationalising education to render it more inclusive and cater for those who may not be very academically inclined. A report emerged from the work of the committee titled; "Learning to do: Towards learning and working society."

In 1986, the then Prime Minister Rajiv Gandhi, sought to move the system towards educational principles and policies that were learner-friendly while also equipping Indian students with a robust scientific temper.

Moves were accordingly initiated to design a curriculum that reflected the chief strengths of a multilingual, multi-ethnic, multicultural country- which is how India has always been. In his broadcast to the nation on evolving a curriculum in tune with the scientific, technological and economic advancement of India, Rajiv Gandhi observed.

> "... I would strongly emphasise education's organic link with the productive forces of society. We shall reorganise vocational education to align it with industry, agriculture, communications and other productive sectors of the economy." (1986, p. 5)

The then education minister followed it up with a status report titled "Challenges of education: A policy perspective." This had important ramifications. In 1986, the Ministry of Human Resources Development brought out a document titled- 'National Policy on Education, 1986: A presentation.' This initiated a lot of debates in Parliament, leading to the creation of National Policy on Education. The policy thus formulated had the following observations to make:

(a) Regardless of the institute, school or college or the resources or framework of a policy, the eventual determinant of success or failure is determined by society and the cooperation of the stakeholders. There must be a purpose, goal and aim, and enough commitment is a pre-requisite for the success of the course.

(b) The vital ingredient determining the success of a plan is implementation; it is therefore of the essence to put in placing a plan where resource allocation and the teaching learning process are guaranteed to succeed.

(c) The goals of the education policy need to be unambiguously defined and every member involved in the mission should pull his weight to get the mission to come to fruition.

(d) Both resources and the moves to restructure the education system need to be commensurate with the policies laid out as part of curriculum revision.

(e) The two massive stumbling blocks to effective change in policy are resource constraint and resistance to change. These need to be tackled at the grassroots level. Curriculum designers, subject experts, managers and teachers need to put their heads together and "lay down the prerequisites and parameters of implementation so that the hard work, innovation and truly imaginative idealism of the stakeholders do not go waste."

(f) The purpose of education is to inform and enlighten. The eventual idea is a learning society that has at its heart the removal of ignorance and the entry of vibrance. Thus, in addition to formal education open, non-formal, part time and adult education needs to be encouraged and strengthened.

(g) Education is a national responsibility; only those who have interests of the nation at heart would ever see the restorative function performed by education. There must be very amicable centre-state relations and a shared responsibility involving everyone connected directly or indirectly with education.

(h) Finally, education is the only way to develop India's human resources intellectually.

In terms of Teacher and Teacher Education, the following points which were observed in 1989-1990 are relevant even to this day.

(i) There is a good deal of politicisation in teacher's organisations. (1988, p. 21).

(ii) Much of teacher education is irrelevant.

(iii) The selection procedures and recruitment systems for teachers have not kept pace with the needs in terms of either number or of quality.

(iv) Teaching has become the last choice in the job market.

(v) Adequate attention has not been made to develop communication skills which are crucial to the functioning of teachers.

(vi) The training programme does not make use of audio-visual equipment.

(vii) Teachers in the training colleges are not exposed to the ideas of national integration, cultural cohesion and development of humanitarian values.

(viii) Many teachers do not get any opportunity to keep themselves abreast with technical aids for more effective teaching.

(ix) There is a good deal of politicisation in teacher's organisations.

The committee also made several valid and topical observations on various educational issues *inter-alia* include the following:

(a) Even though the rural areas account for three-fourth of population, they are getting much less by way of resources for education than the urban areas.

(b) The quality and maintenance of school and college buildings in urban areas is very much better than in rural areas.

(c) The dropout rates among urban children are lower than in the rural areas.

(d) Privately managed "quality" institutions are generally located in urban areas.

(e) Despite considerable acceleration in recent years, girl's education is still far behind the boys.

(f) Fewer girls seek admission to professional courses, other than pertaining to medicine, teacher training and nursing.

(g) The spread of education among the girl's students of scheduled castes and scheduled tribes has not been as much as among the male members of the group.

(h) For about 90 per cent of the labour force educational activities have not been organised keeping in view their role and responsibilities.

(i) Three major expert bodies at the national level namely, National Council of Educational Research and Training (NCERT), the National Institute of Educational Planning and Administration (NIEPA) and the University Grants Commission (UGC) have not met with the expected response.

(j) It appears that things have gone awry due to progressive centralisation and bureaucratisation and non-enforcement of discipline standards and performance norms.

(k) The share of elementary education in fund allocation has gone down considerably. From 56 per cent in the first plan it has gone down to 36 per cent in the Sixth plan whereas the share of University education went up from 9 to 16 per cent.

(l) In the total expenditure on education, private donations and endowments accounted for nearly 29 percent at the beginning of this century but declined to the level of 3 percent in 1980-81.

(m) Education has till now been now essentially the responsibility of the states. This means the availability of educational facilities has been dependent not upon the commitment of the nation as a whole, but upon the vicissitudes of the resources allocated by States.

Subsequently, in contrast, the facet of teacher education can be observed from a broader view, which gives space for the teachers to make informed choices. The emphasis in teacher education is more on developing individual (teacher's) skills so that he/she can adhere to and function in any situation. To quote:

> Teacher education programmes were seen as being responsible for producing teacher of a high calibre. The main function of these programmes was to hope generate professional skills in the teacher. [Sic] (Larsen-Freeman, 1983: 265)

Here one recalls the words of Dr Warren:

> Teacher preparation requires programmes that maintain a necessary balance between research–based knowledge and professional practice schools. Teacher must be made an expert in content, methodology and evaluation. They must know what they are teaching, how to teach it and be able to detect to what extent it has been learnt by the pupils. Teacher must be a school professional of great skills and ability. Teacher education must generate such skills. (Vedantam, 1998).

The strand 'Education' is a measured learning process in which the learner (teacher) is of utmost importance in language teaching. The component, Training may bring about learning. Nevertheless, it may not bring about a change in the learner (Teacher). Education is said to be something more than the acquisition of practical skills. The element of 'Training tends to convergence and a reliance on established technique,' while 'education tends toward divergence and a readiness to break from prescribed practices' (Widdowson, 1983)

It may be observed that three models of teacher education are proposed by Wallace (1991). These are - The craft model, the applied science model, and the reflective model.

2.4. The Craft Model

As per the craft model, trainee teachers acquire mastery of the skills by observing and listening to instruction like an apprentice learning by imitation and a careful replication of his master's action. Not astonishingly, this model is unable to accommodate advances in knowledge. Implicit in this model is the passive or the receptive role of the trainees. They are not to question the knowledge content, the teaching methodology or classroom strategy of the trainer. The flow chart given below explains the process in this model.

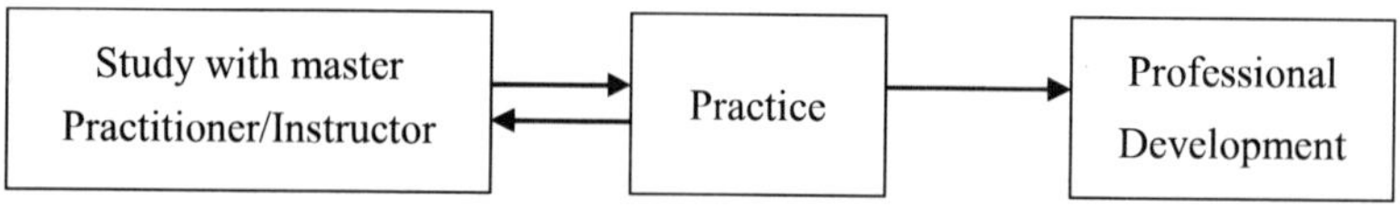

(Wallace 1991:6)

2.5. The Applied Science Model

This model advocates the application of received knowledge and subjects it to regular experimentation so as to refine the received knowledge. Constant experimentation leads to refinement and development. The task of the trainers is to expand the knowledge of the trainees. It follows that the trainees' sharpness in this theoretical knowledge would turn out to be excellent at applying this knowledge – to attain solutions for various issues in their classroom practice.

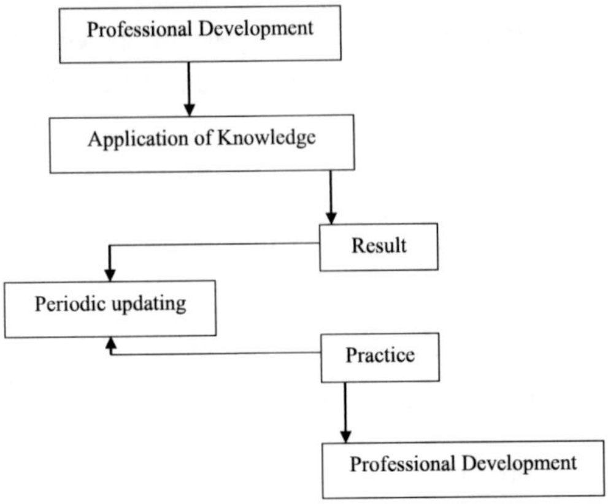

(Wallace 1991:9)

2.6. The Reflective Model

The most influential model demonstrated in the present area of study is the one developed in Wallace 1991. The reflective model relies on Schon's postulates of four constants which reflecting teachers bring to their reflection:

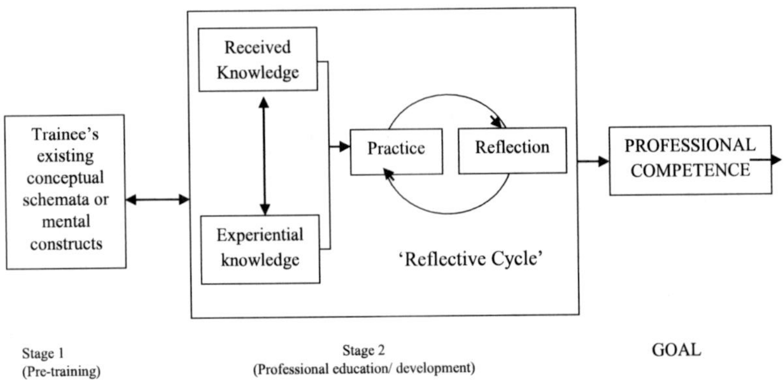

(Wallace 1991:15; 49)

The main criticism yet again of teacher education is that the process of teacher preparation is largely controlled by an 'expert'. Factors like teacher experience, teacher personality, and teacher attitudes do not seem to get adequate attention. To accommodate these factors, teacher education was extended to teacher development. Moreover, it has been opined that '...Development...focus on the individual teacher can lead to do a better job and to personal and professional growth...' (Freeman, 1982:21-22)

2.7. Models of Teacher Development Programmes

Breen and others undertook a study on teacher development programmes for eight years and framed three models of teacher development programmes – out of three phases – they evolved in their study (Breen et al., 1989: 111). They are:

(a) The transmission model: This is like traditional method of teaching and learning. In this model trainers or teacher educators are prime sources of information, innovations and solutions for teaching-learning problems. As teachers are passive recipients, they will be loaded with all know-how. The main purpose of this model is to convince the teachers about the correctness of the principles, techniques or innovations and urge them to engage in critical evaluation of their classroom practices and to adapt them to the rationale behind a given reform programme. As the time for the programme is restricted, the teacher educators expect changes to come about in teachers. There is no possibility to check the new method or technique in real classroom environment and in teaching-learning context. The criticism against this model is that there is no provision to extend the programme to understand practical problems of implementation of new know-how. Another is that teachers fail to pay good attention as they experience issues under discussion in their daily classroom interactions. The principal source of change and development is the expertise of the trainer. The expertise drives primarily though not from the theory and research resources other than classroom practices (*Ibid;* 117).

(b) Problem-solving model: This model focuses on the problems that are faced by the teacher in the teaching-learning context. This model deals with active interaction between the teacher on the one hand and experts, a group of teachers and the problem on the other hand. The experts are consultants in this model. The main purpose of this model is finding solutions to the problems identified by the teachers in their classrooms. It enables the teacher to understand his or her students and their requirements for better learning. In the process of finding solutions they share information with other teachers and enrich their knowledge base and sensitivity towards various problems for learning in different contexts. The teacher's attitude and the way of handling the different classroom situations will be developed when they receive suggestions, ideas, solutions, techniques and plans for classroom procedures from the experts and group of teachers. Breen says,

> that this type of development programmes will establish a new cycle…where the search for solutions related to teacher problems and learner work serves as a basis for workshops. Through practical application and subsequent sharing of experience from implementation, more precise problems and issues could be identified for later workshops (*Ibid,* 122).

Teachers go back to their classes to test the solutions in their action research whether they are suitable or whether they would they generate counter-problems in the particular context. If they give rise to another problem, it can be subject matter for the next teacher development programme. Breen found another benefit of this model. It facilitates the formation of small working groups of teachers.

> *The teachers began to initiate and co-operate in action research in their own classrooms and share their discoveries with their colleagues… participants carried out plans for the documentation and later analysis of classroom work. Such documents included observations schedules, teacher diaries, collections of samples of pupils' work and pupil evaluation of both their own work and of several aspects of the classroom process (Ibid, 124).*

Breen opines that though this model ensures teacher development to some extent – still it suffers some drawbacks. They are:

(i) All teachers are not able to articulate their experiences in the form of problems for discussion. They just reserve themselves to the talk and observe the events passively between the particular teacher and the expert along with other teachers.

(ii) Though teachers share the information among themselves still the role of expert who will not have any direct connection with the students in the classroom is dominant.

(iii) The period of time of the teacher development programme will not be sufficient to address the issues of every teacher.

(iv) The Classroom Decision-Making and Investigating Model: This model gives more autonomy to the teachers. It is formed on the belief that two classroom situations are neither similar nor have a single solution. The solutions given by experts and group of teachers may not be fit to the classroom of the concerned teacher. The problem may be unique in the particular classroom situation.

This model suggests the training as classroom decision-making and investigation puts the trainer in a team both with participating teachers and the teachers' own learners. Trainers are facilitators within the team, assisting a dialogue between themselves, teachers and their learners (*Ibid.*, 127). The main purpose of this model is to identify the need for innovation in a particular classroom context and explore the possibility of innovation through open interaction and sharing of decision-making between the participants in that context. Trainer will encourage the teachers to take up research projects, observations, investigations and evaluation of actual classroom occurrences and relate these findings to a relevant theory or research. In fact, innovations emerge from the classroom context. This model functions through small teacher development groups which are coordinated by workshops with specific intervals.

> The development programmes and the workshops are the means for participants to propose innovations and to pursue them in practice... Various types of documented classroom work are shared and discussed so that links can be made between an individual's experience of innovation or investigation and generalisable conclusions and principles (*Ibid.,* 130).

Teacher is expected to maintain the documents like teaching dairies, classroom events and peer observations to enable others to understand on which grounds the decisions and theories were made. This model demands teacher responsibility to focus on the problems and needs of his/her pupil for better learning. It brings a change in the process of solving the problems. The current approach and objectives of many programmes are to empower the teacher and learner and labour towards this framework of their autonomy.

> The teacher will have to make his or her own decisions, and he or she will have to do so in the light of a general appreciation of factors that may make a difference, combined with a pretty clear idea of what he is doing and why. (Barrow, 1984:255)

In this particular context, teacher is not in a position to make sound judgments for their classroom situations. Some teachers are not capable enough to identify the problem, making a decision and trying different ways in their action research without involvement of other teachers and experts. So, this model serves better to improve teacher's autonomy in making decisions, identifying problems and finding solutions for their own classrooms. This model ideally connects the experts with the teachers and their students in the classroom. This model takes all the industry of learning into the particular context to give practical training to the teacher to empower himself/herself with subject knowledge and practical experience with coordination of other teachers and experts in addition to replicate the process of making decision, identifying the problem to solve on his/her own. It may be observed that the teacher is a researcher in his/her field of education. The above mentioned model of teacher development ultimately turns teacher-centered class into learner-centered class. The collaborative work of experts with the teachers and their students will strengthen the teachers' ability to formulate hypothesis and test the hypotheses which further can be developed as concrete theories.

2.8. Classroom-centred research in pedagogy

The three essentials of education: research, teaching, and development go hand in hand. They are interrelated. Allwright examines the possible forms of relationship between research, teaching and development and criteria to any proposal for teacher-research (Allwright, 1991). He further opines that research must not be added to the problems that the teacher usually faces, but it should be integrated with his/her routine pedagogic practices. The advocates of 'teacher as researcher' will explain the potential relation between research, teaching and development by adopting any one of the three major positions.

2.9. Research as an (optional) extra

The 'Teacher-researcher' believes that research is to be a part of teacher's routine life. The teacher-researcher must share his/her portion in the whole research enterprise with his/her involvement in research projects. Making research as an extra burden to their pedagogic work whose rewards are in the individual contribution to knowledge building will not influence any professional growth. The whole purpose of the programmes is to develop teachers' research skills and inform them about the model of the research process. It can be looked at as the process becomes hopeless, if it is disconnected with the realities and practical constraints of the actual life of a teacher.

2.10. Research as the driving force for the development

Research in teachers' life is not only just a contribution to the existing knowledge but also it is a driving force of teachers' personal professional development. The research element is the central to the whole pedagogy itself. It enables the teacher to understand better what is happening in his classroom and how it is to be changed for better teaching and learning context.

2.11. Research as the driving force for development and development as the driving force for research progress

The aspect of research enables the teacher to understand the classroom pedagogy which serves well to both professional development and to the additional aims of the general research progress. It may be opined that a significant development in the general understanding of various participants depends largely on the ability to build upon the individual understanding of various participants in the enterprise. Allwright claims that

> The process might be more successful and meaningful if teachers have colleagues working together might surely be capable of developing a theoretical position of some generality or not limited in relevance to just one teacher's experiences...an academic researcher with access to the theory-building work of many different groups of teachers in many different countries might be able to make connections that result in even more general theory-building (Allwright, 1991).

Subsequently, if the research is the mode of assisting the instructor to understand his/her works more adequately, not just pedagogy – although enhanced – but the need for professional development too will be well served. Every programme for teacher-research must bore in mind that what it articulates to the teacher it is addressing to. Allwright suggests that the programme should present research convincingly to be integrated in his/her teaching-learning context.

Allwright stated the ways how integrating research and pedagogy contribute to the professional development in the following:

(a) This process is used to bring teacher together, and to connect teachers with the learners as well as the academic researchers.

(b) This process initiates teachers to explore that what is relevant to their learners and to themselves.

(c) This integration promotes reflection of teacher on his or her own teaching which generates the motive force for professional development.

(d) It encourages teacher to make every movement of teaching must facilitate learning and reflection on learning experience of his or her students.

Integrating research and pedagogy is to be continuous activity instead clubbing them once or twice. Though this is sound enough in the area of learning and professional development of teacher, it has some problems:

(i) Doing research in the language classroom is time consuming, and makes teachers incompetent to complete the curriculum activities within the stipulated time.

(ii) Learning a new skill requires thorough testing before they will be introduced in the classroom.

Furthermore, Allwright advocates an 'exploratory teaching', which aims to minimize the problems by proposing that the investigative activities should be based on pedagogic activities that both teacher and leaner knew and trust. An 'exploratory teaching' proposes to start with 'puzzles' rather than 'problem' where ever this might help. (Allwright, 1991).

2.12. Integrating research and pedagogy through 'exploratory teaching'

According to Allwright, exploratory teaching is a potentially productive way of integrating research and pedagogy (Allwright, 1991). It involves exploiting already familiar and trusted classroom activities – ways of exploring the things that puzzle teachers and learners about what is happening in their own classrooms (Allwright, 1991). It is specially to deal with the problems that teachers are facing in becoming researches in their classrooms and offering practical way of bringing the research perspective properly in the classroom by avoiding the extra burden on the teacher. It further contributes to both professional development and theory building within and across their teaching period. It is potential to offer teachers a minimum-cost way of integrating research and teaching. The main process of 'exploratory teaching' is using one of the familiar activities to investigate teacher and learner 'puzzles'. It brings the teacher much closer to action research model which focuses on change as a way of investigating classroom learning and teaching. It provides ample opportunity to teachers to have their share in deriving convincing interpretations and contribution to general theory-building while undertaking certain research-based projects.

2.13. Promoting teacher development through research based projects

It may be ascertained that certain research-based projects bring teachers together and each of them would be seriously involved in the process of all the development activities. Furthermore, it would facilitate the progress from below through teacher development even in grim situations. A reform can be unleashed and sustained in a collaborative enterprise by involving all the participants of learning-teaching process at grass-root levels. Various issues, problems, suggestions and alternatives marked at every stage can be discussed in groups – of teachers. This process drifts towards forming teacher development groups. Teachers in and around the place can come together to take their part in the research.

It is at present clear that teacher development programmes are structured on certain models or conceptualisations of teacher development. Therefore, an examination of how different teacher development programmes are structured and what content and methodology is best suited for professional development of teacher may be pursued.

2.1. Designing Teacher Development Programmes

Teachers usually believe that their methods, approaches and techniques are fit to their language learning classroom. Hence they may not expect to change their way of teaching. Prabhu opines that resistance to change among teachers can be overcome by their sense of plausibility if engaged with regard to what constitutes effective teaching and learning activities (Prabhu, 1987). Teacher development programmes should raise teachers' awareness about teaching-learning issues behind innovation and must give opportunity to in-depth analysis. They should enable teacher to form generalised conclusions on the topic and theory derived from the analysis of practice. They should be related to the teachers' existing knowledge and should stimulate them to feel comfortable with new methods or techniques. They should provide various opportunities to examine the issues from every aspect to reveal the underlying principles of proposed change in practice.

The observations should not be limited to particular classroom activity but, must be extended to what they have discovered in actual practice. They should acknowledge the fact that no one solution fits two different situations. So, suggestions to teachers should be 'open' to look at more than one possible solution. The vision, activities, strategies, and methodologies should be effective in bringing change in teachers' perceptions and their attitude towards teaching. Kennedy mentions that normative and re-educative strategies offer the best prospect of bringing about change in behaviour and in allowing active participation of teachers in change (Kennedy, 1987). These strategies require changes to deep-seated beliefs and behaviour. They need a collaborative, problem-solving approach.

It is not only the matter of adoption of specific innovation but also the process of teacher development through which involvement of every individual teacher should be encouraged to go for change and innovation in their teaching-learning environment. As teaching is essentially a behavioural or cognitive activity involving attitudes towards learning, any change strategy should take this complexity into account. The normative and re-educative strategy will affect the change in belief that is necessary for long lasting change in the classroom as it stresses on active participation and involvement of each of the teachers. It is necessary to make use of certain criteria for evaluation of the teacher development programmes to differentiate good programme from bad one.

2.15. Criteria for Evaluating Teacher Development Programmes

Ellis in his 'Embryonic Taxonomy of Teacher Preparation Materials and Practices' states that

> if we are to develop our understanding of teacher preparation further, it will be necessary to decide upon evaluative criteria for making principled selections for the large range of options (Ellis, 1990:36).

Though he did not have clarity upon what criteria he has –he indicated their purpose: that is to differentiate good teacher development programmes from bad ones. Stephen Bax (1995) in his 'Principles for Evaluating Teacher Development Activities' describes the principles of the new model trainee-centred teacher development. According to Bax there are two basic criteria for evaluating any teaching development activities. The first is focusing on the question of how far the trainees have a say in the teacher development programmes and the second focusing on the responsibility for both his/her development and his/her colleagues' development.

A. Content-negotiability

The trainer can offer only an experience of the process but not content that is relevant to trainee needs (Woodward, 1991:136). Hence, the activities in these programmes must be designed mostly on content that is negotiable as the content is not predefined. This multiplies the chances of relevance to the trainees. Experiential approaches to teacher development stress on form of activities that are to be trainee-centered with respect to their content. Woodward described 'loop-input' model which encourages the trainees to 'discover their needs' beforehand and at feed back stage although, this seems to provide the trainees minimal input in terms of content. As a result, some activities should be designed that give more scope for trainees to negotiate and offer the content from their classroom teaching experience to maximize their involvement which further ensures implementation of new ideas and techniques for the long term. The trainee should be given freedom to provide their own context that is adaptable for many teaching situations. The level to which content is negotiable can be determined and this in turn permitting the levels of trainees' input on content is to be considered as a measure to evaluate whether the programme is trainee-centered or not.

B. Transferability

This notion is generated from consideration of teacher as a source of teacher development in his or her own right. Effective teacher development can be seen through interaction among colleagues within the school or region. Follow up is to be done at the teacher's own school. Teachers must be encouraged on their classroom observations, counselling, peer observation and self appraisal. The main objective of all these forms is to attempt and promote sharing of information and skills among teachers and analyze the context and learning behaviour of their subjects to innovate some new process of learning for their students. The trainers should validate each programme as to whether their development programme motivates trainees to maximize their freedom to develop content-negotiation and transfer their knowledge to the benefit of their colleagues. A wide variety of perceptions of the concept of teacher development programmes necessitates establishing a conceptual framework in which certain indicators of professional development can be plotted.

2.16. Indicators of Professional Development

The teacher development programmes are for the professional development of language teachers through the suggestions, discussions, reflections, analyses of the teaching and learning activities, and intermittent intellectual support. It is quite obvious that professional development is the continuous process throughout the tenure of the service of the teachers. Therefore, pinpointing the stage at which professional development takes place and in which form it occurs is a hard nut to crack but it is clear that certain assumptions can be made to find relative characteristics of professional development. They are:

(a) Professional flexibility, innovativeness and competence: The teacher must be able to handle his/her own curriculum, take some decision, handle the material, propose innovation, practice, make particular judgment about how to proceed in the classroom, have clarity over the methodology and activities to be used in his/her own classroom.

(b) Awareness of the latest trends in ELT: The teacher must have knowledge about various methods and theories and techniques and their latest developments along with the knowledge of when and how to use them. He should focus on teacher and learner roles in each method. He must use interactive approach to handle the learners.

(c) Documentation and Monitoring: The teacher must have critical reflection and self-enquiry about his/her teaching by maintaining teaching dairies. He must allow other teachers to observe his/her word directly or through recording.

(d) Participation in development programmes: The teacher must have interest in attending in-service teacher development programmes and refresher courses, research-based projects and workshops etc.

(e) Dissemination through networking workshops: The teachers must participate in a wide range of teacher conferences and subject panels etc. The teacher should become a member of 'teacher development groups' to share their classroom experiences, innovation, problems, and solutions honestly.

(f) Sensitivity to identify classroom problems: The teacher must have due care of his/her students and he/she must have keen observation of the needs and concerns of the students. He/she must be ready to offer all possible sources of help to address the classroom problems.

(g) Indication of research stance: The teacher should incline his heart to undertake small projects. He/she should be willing to conduct action research alone or with the cooperation of his/her colleagues or teachers from other schools.

(h) Knowledge of professional development: The teacher must know what professional development means. He/she must know the ways through which he/she can enrich his subjective knowledge and attitude.

In brief, the characteristic feature of a professionally developing teacher is a capacity for autonomous professional-development through self-systematic self study, study of the work of other teachers and testing of ideas by classroom research procedures. These indicators of professional development are neither complete nor exclusive but they are interdependent.

2.17. Teacher Strategies and Learner Strategies

The notion of teacher strategies is the result of teacher reflection – on their teaching methods. As Graham (1998) suggests, those teachers who have thought carefully about how they learned a language, about which strategies are appropriate for which tasks, are more likely to be successful in developing 'strategic competence' in their students. Hence, it may be assumed that a particular strategy used by a teacher, say, putting questions to students in order to elicit responses, may result in students breaking up a unit into manageable chunks that can be learnt using the question-answer method. Similarly, in a classroom that encourages students to reflect on their learning styles, the teacher may use the strategy of learner reflection to inform his/her learners about the benefits of certain learning styles.

It becomes crucial for teachers to study their teaching context, with special care on learning styles of students and the materials used for teaching. To adopt a strategy or a set of strategies for teaching learners, a teacher has to know something about the learners, their interests, motivations, learning styles, etc. This awareness in turn would help a teacher recast his/her lesson plans in such a manner that learners can learn the language that is being modelled, presented or practised by the teacher. This applies to a teacher–centered classroom; a specific number of tasks that provide students with opportunities to use and develop their Language Learning Strategies (LLS) may be used. Learner strategies are broadly defined as

> ...specific actions, behaviours, steps or techniques that students (often intentionally) use to improve their progress in developing L2 skills. These strategies can facilitate the internalisation, storage, retrieval or use of the new language. Strategies are tools for the self- directed involvement necessary for developing communicative ability. (Oxford, 1990)

It has come to light that language learning strategies (LLS) and language strategy training are possible and many L2/FL classes try to achieve precisely this in the latter. It is in this context that learning strategies have to match teaching strategies.

2.18. Use of Mother Tongue as a strategy to teach L2 and some other related aspects

English language teachers and learners have been concentrating on target language, i.e., L2. Language is seen as a communicative tool and not as a system, where L1 and L2 are two parts of that tool especially in English Language Teaching. An attempt will be made to see how L1 is utilised positively or negatively across different language teaching methods.

Use of L1 across language teaching method has established or recognised English as a foreign Language (EFL) – teaching methods either minimized the role of the L1(Howatt, 1984:212) or adopted the avoidance of the L1, called by (Stern, 1992) as 'the integral strategy'. Here language is used as a grammar translation method (GTM). Hence, in this method the mother tongue is used as a medium of instruction (Byram, 2004). In other words, it has been noted that 'the first language is mentioned as a reference system in the acquisition of the second language' (Stern, 1983:455). It is assumed that a formal learning of the rules of L2 grammar by contrast to those of the L1 grammar helps to master the language.

> If... the mother tongue is a central element in the process of learning a foreign language, why is it so conspicuously absent from the theory and methodology of the communicative approach? Why are so little attention paid in this and other aspects, to what learners already know? (Swan, 1985: 86).

Atkinson (1987) integrates communicative methodology with selective and limited use of L1 and noted that it is impossible to talk of a 'right balance' or a perfect model for using L1 and it's not that simple. L1 can be a valuable resource for if used at appropriate times and in appropriate ways.

N.S. Prabhu (1987) in his task based language teaching (TBLT) or the communicational teaching project (CPT) encouraged the use of one's own linguistic resources to some problems, and allowed the use of such strategies as using simple words, resorting to gestures, quoting from the black board or the sheet which stated the bask, seeking a suggestion from peers, even using the mother tongue/ L1. He takes an impartial view in this regard, and does not completely ban or fully allow the use of L1. His position is in the middle of the pendulum.

2.19. Teacher Development in the Indian context

A teacher's job can never remain stagnant. She or he has to constantly evolve and augment knowledge in an attempt to impart current information to her or his students. Unfortunately the system of school education is so demanding and rigorous that a teacher hardly has time or energy to concentrate on personal development. It is ironic to note that teachers become so involved in educating their students that they neglect personal growth, and that they very soon find that while their efforts as good teachers have helped students to settle down in very lucrative and successful careers, it has generally been at the cost of sacrificing their own professional growth. Without doubt teachers feel proud when their students excel but it is also sometimes pathetic to find teachers who have remained stagnant which may result in bitterness and envy. A teacher needs to be one step ahead of the students in expertise and knowledge. Therefore, it is essential for teachers to be more prospective and concentrate on improving and enhancing their academic assets. School administrations should also realise that training and development of teachers from time to time is essential to infuse new vigour, fresh dimension and to be concurrent with recent development in the relevant field. Efforts to facilitate personal development of teachers will result in development of their students, school and society at large. The terms Teacher Training, Teacher Education and Teacher Development though apparently very similar at face value are in reality quite distinct from one another. It is imperative to differentiate between their shade of meaning and uniqueness.

Widdowson (1983) and Richard and Nunan (1990) consider Teacher Training as being more involved with 'familiarising student teachers with techniques and skills to apply in the classroom' Rama Mathew (2015:29). Teacher Training focuses on training teachers and orienting them to teach using tested techniques in order to bring freshness to the class and yield better result. As part of its effort to improve standards and refresh teachers, APSCHE (Andhra Pradesh State Council of Higher Education) had initiated a three day Train the Trainer programme for its college teachers at Warangal. Some incentives may be provided to teachers to encourage them to register for Teacher Training programmes.

Teacher Education is more continuous and involves concentrated efforts undertaken by teachers to develop and study successful plans of action, evolve theories based on their success and critically analyze and evaluate their performance as a teacher in order to constantly improve and evolve themselves. The teacher is constantly involved in educating oneself based on her or his personal experiences, and sharing the same with other teachers. 'They would like to be uptodate in their subject, but in-service programmes don't seem to help them with this, nor with how to become better teachers; they have to themselves find ways of doing this.' (Pickering and Gunashekar, 2014: 31).The National Council of Teacher Education (NCTE) in its 2009 manifesto recommended the need to encourage education of teachers through shared information and experiences on a common platform. These experiences were expected to yield results in terms of mutual exchange of ideas and experiences.

Teacher Development is by contrast a more voluntary practice. Developmental exercises would involve reflection, experimentation, application, theorising and dissemination of result oriented approaches and practices. The conclusion arrived at by the study carried out by CBSE-ELT curriculum implementation study during 1993 to 1997; unpublished final report by Central Institute of English and Foreign Languages is noteworthy in this regard. The five year project involved teachers in the role of objectively observing their own and their colleagues' classroom interaction. The teacher took on multiple roles ranging from mentors to resource persons, material writers as per requirement and supplemented their knowledge by conducting regular workshops. The project after an in-depth study arrived at a conclusion recommending 'that a top-down as well as a bottom-up approach to curriculum renewal is important to bring about change in schools' (Pickering and Gunashekar, 2014:32) and encouraged the practice of 'an insider-oriented monitoring and evaluation' by 'outside experts' for 'meaningful' and 'sustainable' development. The project however had to be shelved due to paucity of time and funds. Trace study in its report lauded the role of teachers as researchers during monitoring and evaluation and 'underlined the need for building on existing school/Board structures to support the teacher in her on-going professional development.' (Pickering and Gunashekar, 2014:33).

The objective of the Mentoring in Delhi schools A UKIERI in-service project by Central Institute of Education carried out between 2008 and 2010 was to bring teacher education institutes and schools in close contact with one another for better interaction and sharing of information. The project was initiated to develop a programme of mentoring and a supportive teacher body. The study concluded that mere self motivation was not sufficient and teachers had to be encouraged to be ready and available to work beyond their school timings and schedule in order to develop themselves.

A three month study involving ten teachers in Delhi who volunteered to maintain a diary and record their observations and also observe the diary noting of other teachers arrived at the conclusion in a paper presented and published in Innovation in English Language Teacher Education, edited by Pickering and Gunashekar. The teachers felt that their diary noting and observation has helped them to evolve from being descriptive to dialogic in their approach.

It is, therefore, important to encourage teachers to engage in practice teaching and develop a theory based on the results arrived at in the practice teaching sessions. This kind of approach allow teachers access to each other's experience and enrich themselves when they share their findings related to their experiments and corresponding results. These Teacher Development Programmes can build a storehouse of tested and tried out successful strategies with access for other teachers to bank upon.

Padwad and Dixit (2014) hold up the mirror to 'inadequate and ineffective pre-service education'. They further added, Continuing professional development (CPD).

> is ideally viewed as an ongoing process of learning, both formal and informal, after teachers enter the profession...CPD should enable teachers to explore, reflect on and develop their practice, deepen their knowledge of the academic discipline, research and reflect on learners and their education...break out of intellectual isolation and share experiences and insights with others in the field.

One of the most important points that Padwad and Dixit (2014) mention is that the 'state-led large-scale CPD programmes are unlikely to have any impact unless teachers find something personally meaningful and relevant in them'. In addition, they feel that 'the success of large-scale in-service training programmes depends on how far they allow teachers to translate common uniform prescriptions into personally relevant ideas and action plans'.

Padwad and Dixit (2014), without mincing words, clearly state in the preceding paragraph that 'large-scale' programmes would not deliver the results the administration/management expects unless the participant teachers feel those inputs are significant while teaching students.

Sen (2002) in her article, 'Understanding Teacher's Professional Growth through their articulation of Personal Practical Knowledge' explores the possible methods which can be used to help in-service teachers express and share their concerns and experiences as teachers. Besides, she offers suggestions saying that practicing teachers could analyze their 'narratives' and find a 'voice' to record their development in terms of teaching.

In the secondary school curriculum of AP/TSWREIS English is taught and teachers also accept it, therefore a lot of importance is placed on the English language. The teachers' proficiency in English is a precondition to develop English language skills in the learners. Therefore, the government of Andhra Pradesh issued an order in 2003 that those teachers, who wish to apply for the position of an English teacher at secondary schools of APSWREIS, must possess a BA/MA in English literature and should have opted for English methodology in B.Ed. Even the NCF (2005: 108) lays emphasis on this particular aspect. There is a fundamental defect in this type of policy. The BA English literature curriculum in Andhra Pradesh concentrates more on English literature and less on the language components. However, literature teachers do not discuss anything about English language from the language perspective. The B.Ed. English methodology lays emphasis on teaching methods/approaches curriculum development, language evaluation and other pedagogical topics. Therefore, the APSWREIS has been conducting programmes to improve their proficiency levels in English and also to teach their learners effectively. If we try to address the issue of preparing efficient English language teachers the answer in metaphorical terms is:

> we are a solitary lamb lost in a dark and damp wilderness. When others are talking about world class education, we are still grappling with issues of teaching English to English teachers – a rather sad and a formidable situation (Devupalli, 2012).

The practicing English teachers of APSWREIS need subject matter knowledge, and pedagogical knowledge, besides proficiency in English. The manner in which this study was conducted is presented in the next chapter.

Chapter - 3

Evaluation of Teacher Development Programmes

Teacher development programmes (TDPs) were organised by APSWREIS for their English teachers in the erstwhile Andhra Pradesh. TD Programmes are evaluated to find out the extent to which the objectives of APSWREIS are achieved. We have investigated the impact of Teacher Development Programmes on teachers' professional growth and in-service teacher training engagement with classroom practices. In addition to this, it made an effort to outline the impact of TD programmes organised by APSWREIS and subsequently, the main objective of the study to consider how TD measures are treated in one area of endeavour – in the domain of ELT. The study was based on the primary objective to determine to what extent the current TD Programmes facilitate the development of teachers' skills and how effective teacher development programmes are. We have found answers to the following questions:

(i) Do the objectives of teacher development programmes match with the needs and expectations of the teachers (with specific reference to the English component) of APSWREIS?

(ii) Are the teachers' views and learning reflected in actual classroom practice?

Data was collected in four phases. In the first phase, a questionnaire was given to the academic coordinator, to establish whether they received any inputs regarding training programmes and what kind of input teachers received through TD training programmes. In the second phase, semi-structured interviews were conducted for 15 resource persons to know about the problems resource persons and teachers faced in fulfilling APSWREIS objectives, and to know whether the training programmes incorporated the recent trends in ELT, and to know whether these training programmes were helpful in generating awareness about approaches, methods and materials to be used in the APSWREIS curriculum. In the third phase, two questionnaires (open and closed ended) were administered to teachers to understand whether teachers were given inputs about students' socio-economic background, if they were sensitised to students' socio-economic background and the measures they employ to take students' background into account. These two questionnaires to express their perceptions of teacher development programmes which they attended periodically – and in their opinion what could be included in teacher development programmes. In the fourth phase, teachers' real classroom practices were recorded to see the teachers' mode – how they are teaching. An observation was undertaken to know whether the inputs that they got from TDPs were useful in their regular mode of teaching, and to know whether TDP inputs are reflected in the English language classroom. The overall plan and procedures followed for this four phase study are presented below in the form of a table.

Table - 1: Details of the four-phase study

Phase	Activity	Tools / Materials Used	Target group	Total
1.	Administration of a questionnaire to Academic coordinator	Questionnaire	Academic coordinator	1
2.	Conducting semi-structured interviews to Resource persons	Semi-structured interviews	Resource persons	15
3.	Administration of a questionnaire to teachers	2 Question-naires (Closed Ended) (Open Ended)	Teachers	30
4.	Teachers' regular classroom teaching observation (three classes for each teacher)	2 Observation checklists	Teachers	30 classes (10 teachers x 3 classes each)
		Video Analysis	Teachers	

3.4. Case Study

We have followed the case study method, which allows the possibility to examine a particular programme in a thorough mode (Merriam, 1998; Stake, 1995; Yin, 2009). Following this, through opinions and semi-structured interviews with the resource persons who taught in the TDPs and the academic coordinator/administrator managing the programmes, and the involvement of APSWREIS teachers in the programme (presenting their responses in the questionnaires), it seemed probable to merge together a valuable overview of the TD programmes. To generate this overview, the study in addition analyses APSWREIS Documents; and undertook Video Recording of actual classroom teaching, and the resource material employed in the training of teachers.

The study method permits a complete investigation of TD programmes and provides some specific features. The method allows the investigator to be part of the programme. Understanding APSWREIS as an institution involved gathering data concerning several individuals and aspects—a detailed analysis that the case study method enables. All the data gathered was in order to generate a careful interpretation and understanding of APSWREIS. This particular method of case study provided for the triangulation of data, an essential module of qualitative investigation (Merriam, 1998). It has been mentioned by Stake (1995) that "it is true that we deal with many complex phenomena and issues for which no consensus can be found as to what really exists—yet we have ethical obligations to minimize misrepresentation and misunderstanding" (p. 108). Merriam further adds the necessity of the triangulation of data, which is assessing from various viewpoints to achieve a better idea of what is in fact taking place. In the present study, the semi/structured interviews with resource persons, collection of responses through questionnaires from the teachers and classroom observation allowed the researcher to examine the situation from various angles.

3.2. Multi-site Case Study Approach for the Present Study

Multi-site case study integrates multiple cases in the same context. As the study involved English teachers working in APSWREIS, it was considered appropriate and methodologically sound to examine them in their natural setting. Subsequently, it was found that there are schools functioning under the Society in different places in the then Andhra

Pradesh. It was required to study teachers working in various schools running under APSWREIS. This could be achieved through a multiple case modeling.

It may be observed that to resolve investigator and single respondent variances in a particular case study (Griffee, 2012), illustrates the incorporation of multiple school - case patterns. Yin (2003) he mentions that the aspect of various cases can deliver "analytic benefits". Therefore, it may be pointed out that replicability is desirable. Nevertheless, there are alternatives of showing approximate variances in the findings from single cases; however the common observations can certainly contribute to significant representations.

It has been asserted by Yin that 'replication' more than 'sampling' is fundamental to the production of multiple school - case patterns. The reason is that replications supplement more consistent findings. On the other hand, the investigator may have to reevaluate the number of variables to be incorporated in the study. In individual case studies, thorough studies of several variables are prompted. Nonetheless, a related method in the case of multiple schools - cases will prove that practicability matters. Yin further opines that all the reproductions ought not to be 'literal replications'. A few cases may be verbatim, others can be hypothetical. If a multiple school - case pattern surveys a suitable replication form, the issue with the number of cases will not be a matter (Yin, 2003, p. 51). Furthermore, the investigator should know whether the investigation will be universal or fixed in nature. Scholz and Tietje (2001) emphasize that an all-inclusive case study is designed by systematic qualitative methodology that depends on description, constructive case studies, comprise more than one unit, or object, of scrutiny and generally are not restricted to qualitative investigation alone. The diversity of data is examined in any case relatively in sub-units, which prioritize various prominent characteristics of the case. (pp. 9-10).

It has been argued by Yin (2009) that the case study method is important when an investigator is probing questions that relate to how or why a recent occurrence has happened in a specific way. Yin mentions that as an investigative method, "the case study approach is used to contribute to our knowledge of individual, group, organisational, social, political, and related phenomenon. In brief, the case study method allows investigators to retain the holistic and meaningful characteristics of real life events" (p. 4). Hence, when an investigator is concerned with the how and the why of particular situations, aiming at the current conditions, without imposing control of the communicative phenomenon in inquiry, case study method is suitable.

The present study was carried out on the basis of the investigator's previous (Govindaiah, 2004) research undertaken on APSWREIS. The researcher was able to examine the English language teaching aspects applied by the in-service teachers of APSWREIS. The previous study became an opportunity to estimate the strengths and weaknesses of the Society. The earlier study enabled the researcher to get a sense of what problems prevailed in the study as stated by the teachers of APSWREIS, who had started their assignment as qualified teachers of English. The research questions that were probed in the earlier research were as (i) What features of teaching are the in-service teachers of APSWREIS adopting in their instruction as language teachers? and (ii) Which of the teaching methods do the English teachers perceive as suitable and what inconsistencies did they face in T D Programmes?

Semi structured interviews with resource persons were conducted. The earlier study included questionnaires to teachers who had been teaching WLA (Whole Language Approach) efficiently for more than 3 years. The teachers expressed their views on T D programmes that they sensed were beneficial, and some of the strategies in which they believed they were untrained. The findings of the earlier study point out that there is greater need for T D programmes. The resource persons felt that in-service teachers were to be motivated through training programmes to demonstrate responsiveness in their real time teaching and to perceive themselves as researchers. The resource persons noticed that they wanted their teacher participants to visualise themselves as enthusiastic representatives of their learners while dealing with WLA – a holistic model and a systematic study of language. The recommendations originating from the study argued for the requirement of an independent WLA teacher preparation in the language education programme that would need enhanced interaction between the resource persons and the participants where in-service teachers would attain real time student teaching skill.

As opposed to simply employing the comments collected through the semi Structured interviews organised for the resource persons, classroom observation permitted a first-hand understanding into how the teaching functions in actual practice. Furthermore, the study comprised analysis APSWREIS documents, responses given by the in-service teachers through questionnaires and the observation – video-recording of the real time classroom environment which allowed the researcher to examine the teachers' ability. This method determines how teachers are implementing the skills that they have gained through TD Programmes in their work as qualified English teachers.

The aspect of qualitative exercise, in regard to case study, may be said to be challenging to define in precise terms. It has been noted that one preferred aspect of case study is research stratagem where the queries 'how' or 'why' may be posed, when the researcher has little command over occurrences, and when the priority is on a present factor surrounded by some actual-life context (Yin, 2003, p.1). In an applied linguistic background, a case study can be employed for examining a specific case which can be a teacher, a learner, a class, an institution or a group.

In second language conditions, it is time and again employed for pursuing language improvement, recounting interpositions, comprehending and evaluating a specific case, etc. (McKay, 2006). In-depth investigation, context-selectivity, association of individual features and singularity are more or less the essential elements of a case study (Duff, 2007). On the other hand, apart from the definite nature (descriptive) of research questions, as mentioned by Johnson (1992, p. 91)

> ...a case must have a thorough report of the research framework, the justification for the selection of members and a meticulous description of their profile, the hypothetical positioning of the study, the presumed part of the investigator, a thick description of the measures of data collection, scrutiny and findings of the study, and an overview on the rationality and significance of the study.

3.3. The Site of APSWREIS

The study was undertaken through a stratified random sampling of schools that are run under the management of APSWREIS, located in various districts of the then United Andhra Pradesh. The schools selected are located in urban, semi-urban and rural areas. There were some limitations too in the process of evaluation in the study of APSWREIS. Though the institution does undeniably reach a good number of in-service teachers, this number is outnumbered by the number of state government school teachers that they do not cater for. Consequently, it may be noted that although most of in-service teachers of APSWREIS who do attend TD programmes, are aware of the importance and its credibility, there are many who still cannot cope with the programme standards. APSWREIS has organised a number of TD programmes, and while it is one that is maintaining standards, it also has its limitations and cannot coordinate more than what it is programmed to. APSWREIS organises TD programmes for in-service English teachers that run for 4 - 14 days. One of the agendas of this research was to study the 04 - 14 day programmes; they were documented during 2007 – 2014. The travel and lodging expenses of the participants are borne by APSWREIS when they come for the TDPs. The state government funds and supports TD Programmes. The campuses in which the programmes were organised by The English and Foreign Languages University (EFLU), Hyderabad (2007; 2012; 2013); Don Bosco Navajeevan Campus Hyderabad (2012); The Andhra Pradesh Academy of Rural Development (APARD) Hyderabad (2013).

3.3. The Participants

Data was collected from three types of respondents: Participants: Resource Persons, Academic Coordinator and in-service teachers who attended TD Programmes. As the investigator began his study, he approached the Academic Coordinator of APSWREIS. The investigator informed him of the research, its objectives, time frame, and the requirements, and told him that all information collected for the study would be kept confidential. After obtaining permissions from the authorities concerned, the investigator commenced the study. The Academic Coordinator and the Resource persons were incredibly open and positive in their response to the study. Most of the Resource Persons were ready to offer any support needed and took out time in their schedules for semi-structured interviews with regard to the participants in the research and the organisation of TD Programmes by APSWREIS.

Table - 2: Details of the Academic Coordinator of APSWREIS

S. No.	Type of Coordinators	Organisation
1	Academic Coordinator	APSWREIS

Table - 3: TEACHER DEVELOPMENT PROGRAMMES ORGANIZED BY APSWREIS

S. No.	Organised at University/Institute	Place	Year
1.	The English and Foreign Languages University (EFLU)	Hyderabad	2007
2.	The English and Foreign Languages University (EFLU)	Hyderabad	2012
3.	Don Bosco Navajeevan Campus	Hyderabad	2012
4.	The English and Foreign Languages University (EFLU)	Hyderabad	2013
5.	The Andhra Pradesh Academy of Rural Development (APARD)	Hyderabad	2013

Most of the Resource Persons were professors and experts in English language teaching who were called from various universities and institutes from all over India and almost all of them are experts in teaching English at various levels. As resource persons, they seemed well-versed in their fields, passionate and energetic. They appeared to be striving for a mission (developing teachers) and liked their work. The in-service teachers of APSWREIS on TD programmes were advised to attend the programmes. Consequently, the investigator requested/invited the resource persons and the in-service teachers to become participants in the study. A few of the resource persons and teachers agreed to take part in the investigation. However, the investigator waited to interview the Resource persons and collect opinions from the teachers through questionnaires (closed and open ended) near the conclusion the TD programmes so that they would be competent to speak on the advantages and disadvantages of TD programmes. Hence, during the time taken for data collection, the investigator had to maintain cordial relations with in-service teachers. After several reminders, data was gathered from the participants. Many a Resource person offered his/her time to be interviewed.

Over time, the investigator also approached in-service teachers after the completion of the sessions in common areas like library to ask them if they would be interested in sharing their views. On an overall basis, the investigator interviewed more than 20 resource persons and collected opinions of 40 in-service teachers. However, the data analyses undertaken for the study was limited to 15 Resource persons' semi-structured interviews and 10 in-service teachers' views given through questionnaires for qualitative analysis. The participants were informed of the objectives of the study undertaken by the investigator and introduced to the research questions. Subsequently, the in-service teachers were requested by the investigator for recording (audio-video) their real-time classroom teaching at their working place. As agreed upon to keep the names of participants confidential, no names have been mentioned in the present study. The details of in-service teachers' who have been selected for the study through the application of stratified random sampling method are as follows:

Table - 4: DETAILS OF SELECTED PARTICIPANTS (IN-SERVICE TEACHERS) FROM THE SCHOOLS RUN BY APSWREIS

S. No.	Designation	Gender	Name of the Area School/District	Type of School
1	TGT	Male	Shaikpet/Hyderabad	(Boys) Magnet
2	TGT	Male	Kondapur/Hyderabad	(Boys) Magnet
3	TGT	Female	Isnapur/Medak	(Girls) Magnet
4	TGT	Male	Achampet/Mahbubnagar	(Boys) RPRP
5	TGT	Male	Madhanapuram/ Mahbubnagar	(Boys) RPRP
6	TGT	Female	Gowlidoddi/Ranga Reddy	(Girls) Magnet
7	PGT	Male	Shaikpet/Hyderabad	(Boys) Magnet
8	PGT	Female	Chitkul/Medak	(Girls) RPRP
9	PGT	Female	Mulugu/Medak	(Girls) RPRP
10	PGT	Male	Chilukuru/Ranga Reddy	(Boys) Magnet

TGT= 4 Male, 2 Female PGT=2 Male, 2 Female

3.4. Description of Cases

The three areas rural, semi-urban and urban are associated respectively with nine schools 2 types (Magnet & RPRP). Magnet school: a school designed to attract pupils from various areas or groups, especially one offering specialist tuition in a particular subject alongside the standard curriculum. **RPRP**: Rural Poverty Reduction Project maintained by APSWREIS, comprised the 26 participants (15 Resource Persons (Training Academic Coordinator), 1 Academic Coordinator, and 10 Teachers,). Consequently, two English teachers from each school were selected to take part in the investigation, which in addition comprised TD programmes aiming to develop their English language teaching ability. The in-service teachers' backgrounds were varied; many came from very semi-urban and rural areas. Some of the teachers were fluent in English. However, there were others who were unable to utter a few sentences in English. Most of the in-service teachers showed enthusiasm in the participating in TD programmes. But, a few said they were at TD programmes because they were compelled to be and did not attend the sessions regularly. Subsequently, the investigator observed that most of the teachers were dedicated and committed. Interviewing the Resource persons, Academic Coordinator and collecting the responses of the teachers involved in the research programme allowed the researcher to grasp what the broad principles of the T D programmes are and how APSWREIS attempted to fulfill those objectives. It further enabled the study to figure out the wider framework, which affects how the Academic coordinator designed and executed T D programmes. The evaluation through video recording supplied documentation of how the teachers incorporate their strategy of language teaching. The investigation of course material, APSWREIS teachers' cultural beliefs, and the recording of the teacher sample lessons permitted the researcher to better comprehend the method to language education being adopted by APSWREIS. Subsequently, the conducting of semi-structured interviews with resource persons and responses collected from in-service teachers permitted the investigator to find how the objectives of the current study are being incorporated and identified.

3.5. Sampling for the Survey

A stratified random sampling method was selected for the investigation undertaken during the third phase of the research. The Researcher met thirty teachers at British Council Conference at Hyderabad, organised by EFL University. Teachers were selected from rural, semi-urban, and urban; teachers were across the 23 districts of the then United Andhra Pradesh. The percentage of the number of English teachers working in APSWREIS schools is equal in proportion in all the districts. Since official information was available about the exact number of English teachers working at the schools that come under the APSWREIS, it was felt that there was no further need to go for a more accurate sample of teachers. It may be stated that one of the tools employed for the investigation was 'questionnaire' (Close Ended & Open Ended). The questionnaire was accepted after going through the research in the related field as elucidated by Stufflebeam (1971a, 2007) and Ellis (1997). They particularly comment on the need for appropriate types of questionnaires utilised for substantive research projects. Joe L. Kincheloe (2012) mentions a related type of questionnaire concerning cultural aspects.

The questionnaire for teachers (see Appendix-III and IV) was designed by the investigator to identify the viewpoints of 10 teachers (who took part in the study), subsequent to their attending TD Programmes. The questionnaire reported 16 categories (8 Close Ended & 8 Open Ended) and 16 of those were intended to obtain teachers' opinions about the strategies they used for self-development in teaching. The first eight categories were employed to acquire information about their capability as well as their opinion of training in teacher development aspects. The rest of the categories were designed keeping in view aspects such as the socio and cultural background of the students, issues relating to overall curriculum and syllabus content, the appropriacy of the materials being used and scope for training in independent materials production, approaches and methods of teaching English, evaluation, teachers' beliefs and leaners' beliefs, action research and research awareness. It must be pointed out at this juncture that these categories were on no occasion intended to be closed sections. Instead, the objective was to make sure smooth and meaningful examination and analysis of the procured information under these categories. In the questionnaire, sections 1, 2, 3, 4 and 5 represented context, syllabus methodology, materials and pedagogy; 6, 7, 8, represented alternative pedagogic support, evaluation and suggestions, which may be said to comprise the category teachers' development strategies. The questionnaire was scored on a five-point Likert scale featuring SA (Strongly Agree), A (Agree), NS (Not Sure), D (Disagree), SD (Strongly Disagree). The teachers had to decide on one of these choices to point out their perception about the statements in the questionnaire. The questionnaire was employed for analysis after it was rated by three University teachers who had a familiarity in instructing MA and Research students at the university level.

3.6. Justification for the Use of the Questionnaire Provided to the Teachers

The teacher questionnaire was used to get the relevant information about the problems teachers faced in the classroom. This tool was designed to know the beliefs of the practicing English teachers as to how teacher development could be fine-tuned to make it need-based. This was necessary as practicing teachers possessed first-hand information about the profile and the needs of English language learners at secondary school level and they act as a link between the language learners and the English language teacher development programmes being offered. The proposed data collection instrument was examined by a panel of experts. The five experts gave their vital inputs regarding the content validity, comprehensiveness and clarity of the tool. This helped the researcher collect accurate and adequate data. The questionnaire has eight sections. All the sections have four internal questions each.

Section A deals with the social and cultural background of the students. It has the internal questions to know if teachers had any input regarding these things; teachers' reaction in dealing with these sensitive issues in the classroom, how they do it in the classroom and whether they expect any kind of these sensitisation inputs in their future programmes.

Section B deals with curriculum and syllabus. In this section, the questions are about aspects of curriculum, syllabus, how they are helpful for teachers, use of supplementary materials, and whether teachers need any crucial inputs on these topics in their future programmes.

Section C gets data about whether teachers received any training on the appropriate use of authentic materials, language culture specific, materials that discuss social issues, and also about the help teacher training programmes provide to teachers to develop materials.

Section D deals with the kind of training teachers got in using different methods in teaching, the usefulness of such methods in classroom, different methods in teaching language skills and aspects and teacher expectations on future training programmes regarding inputs on language skills.

Section E is about evaluation; it asks questions regarding the kind of evaluation practices discussed in training programmes and how effective they are in the classroom and what are the methods and measures the teachers follow in the classroom.

Section F is the most crucial part in this questionnaire; it contains questions about teacher and students beliefs. The questions were whether teacher training programmes focus on teacher and student beliefs about learning and teaching, whether teachers were aware of these concepts, and if discussion of these topics made any difference to their teaching.

Section G is about these teachers' need to conduct research projects, this section sought to know if training programmes helped them in conducting research projects and how far they were useful in taking the classroom related topics and themes to its logical end.

The last **Section H** is about developing research awareness among teachers, and how useful these training programmes are in developing research awareness among teachers in order to carry forward a classroom discussion into a research project.

The questionnaire (see Appendix-I) was designed by the investigator to record the viewpoints of the academic coordinator of APSWREIS and the academic coordinator at EFLU –organisers of the TD Programmes. The questionnaire consisted of 20 questions (14 closed & 6 open-ended) which were intended to receive the organisers' opinions – concerning the strategies of teacher development factors inculcated by TD Programmes to APSWREIS English teachers. The first three questions were employed to acquire information about their experience and capability. The rest of the questions were designed keeping in view the training of the teacher, the infrastructure available for English teachers in APSWREIS, issues relating to overall TD Programmes, the particularities of TD programmes and the observation of teachers in actual classroom situation. The opinions of the participants were recorded and the responses are discussed in the next chapter. The coordinators had to decide on choices that were part of the questionnaire – to point out their perception about the statements in the questionnaire. The questionnaire was employed for investigation after it was validated by three University teachers who had taught masters courses in ELT and guided research in ELT.

3.7. Classroom Audio-Video Recording

Classroom Video-Recording – Class VIII – (3 periods – 10 teachers) was undertaken to analyze teachers' abilities that they have inculcated from TD programmes which they had attended periodically. Three periods per teacher were recorded. This tool was designed to know (i) teachers' performance in teaching, (ii) teachers' interaction with students, (iii) teacher proficiency in language, (iv) teacher preparation with regard to the content to be delivered in the classroom, (v) teaching methods and approaches followed, (vi) pedagogical content knowledge, (vii) socio-cultural background of the student, and (viii) classroom management ability of teachers. The activity was undertaken on the assumption that the teachers have adequate information about effective teaching strategies through English language teaching methodology. Teacher's cultural attitudes and beliefs were taken into account in the project. This aspect of the teacher was important for the development of students in APSWREIS. A panel of experts recommended Audio-Video recording of the proceedings, five experts gave their suggestions regarding classroom observation schedule, comprehensiveness and clarity of the tool used in the study.

3.7.1 Teacher Observation Checklist

The observation schedule of teacher classroom teaching was used as a tool to understand real classroom practice along with a checklist. Observation checklist (see Appendix-VI) was adopted from Gray, Lambert, Centra, et al. (1976). These classes were also used to understand how far training programmes were useful to teachers facing real classroom situation, what their problems were, how teachers used materials, what means they used to develop their own materials according to the needs of students, what methods they followed in teaching, and if these methods were useful to students. These video recorded classes were also used to understand how teachers deal with sensitive issues, whether they follow the principles taught to them in the classroom and if the materials they were using was helpful to them to deal with situations in the classroom. These classes helped the researcher to understand teachers' real problems to enable him develop a suitable model for teacher training programmes at APSWREIS.

3.8. Semi-Structured Interviews

Semi structured interviews were conducted for resource persons to understand what resource persons feel about the fulfilling of objectives of APSWREIS in giving inputs to English language teachers about incorporating recent trends in ELT, and creating awareness about approaches, methods, materials, curriculum and language evaluation as practised in the contemporary classroom. The semi-structured interviews consisted of four questions (see Appendix-II). At the time of interviews some relevant questions were asked. These questions focused on objectives of teacher training programmes, methods, materials, evaluation and recent trends in ELT. They sought information from resource persons about how solutions are given to problems faced by teachers at the time of teaching.

Chapter - 4

Efficacy of Teacher Development Programmes

The present study proposes to know the efficacy of teacher development programmes (TDP) in the context of practicing secondary school English teacher development programmes at APSWREIS in Andhra Pradesh and Telangana regions on the basis of their opinion and the researcher's classroom observation of regular classroom teaching of the teachers. The research attempts to make an examination of the above-mentioned factors so as to suggest ways and means to improve the teacher development programmes. Hence, as mentioned earlier, the aim of the present research is to examine the teacher-problems – while instructing in English medium at APSWREIS. The chapter discusses and presents the analysis of the data that has been collected. The current TDPs have been evaluated through closed-ended questionnaire and questionnaire handed over to the practicing English teachers. Furthermore, a classroom observation schedule to record practicing English teachers' classroom teaching, an open-ended questionnaire for academic coordinator of the APSWREIS and semi-structured interviews for TDP coordinators and resource persons were employed.

Data was collected from one academic coordinator. His role is to conduct training programmes and workshops for the teachers of (subjects) disciplines. Apart from the resource persons and the teachers who attended the TDPs, the Academic Coordinator was also included for this study by the researcher. The coordinator said that he had worked as a language teacher for 12 years, 3 years as a teacher trainer, as a coordinator for 2 years and as a principal for 8 years. Further, he had also attended workshops and seminars on English Language Teaching in the last six years. The aim of the workshops and seminars was to introduce new syllabus, textbooks and new pedagogies in Teaching English. He also mentioned that he had observed his teachers' teaching skills and activities used in the classroom and found that most of them were using traditional methods which were boring and involved less interaction between teachers and students. He further asked his teachers to have more activity-based teaching, use video/audio clips and make classrooms learner-centered in order to break the monotony. The coordinator said that teachers should make their students participate in role plays, debate, pair/ group discussions and presentations.

He further stated that teachers complained about the textbooks that are in use and the due to shortage of materials/textbooks, very few activities were given in the textbooks. There was also shortage of time to do activities in the class. Teachers had not been trained in the methodologies recommended in the textbooks. However, he feels that students like doing activities; they even prefer to listen to their teachers' explanation and showed interest in doing activities by themselves. He also mentioned that measures had been taken to improve the situation. The teacher should not force students to do activities; he also encouraged exchange of experiences through workshops/seminars among teachers engaged in training centers (e.g. colleges/universities). The coordinator further said that APSWREIS had organised training programmes for English language teachers at school, district and regional level. The primary objective of the programmes was to use English as a Second Language (ESL). The duration of the workshop was one day and methodology used in it was interactive/demonstration mode. The criteria for selecting resource persons was passion and resourcefulness. There were follow up activities conducted and the impact of the workshop was very effective and helpful. Further, he observed that the main objective(s) of teaching English in APSWREIS was to empower the teachers to teach and effectively impart the LSRW Skills.

The coordinator further felt that the English language proficiency of APSWREIS's teachers is not up to the mark. In addition to this, he felt that the measures that are to taken to improve the situation are to permit any teacher with competency. Following this, he noted that the APSWREIS provides computer lab, audio, video materials in the school. However, the Academic Coordinator was not satisfied with the use of these materials. He felt that all schools have library facility. Nevertheless, the reading materials and reference materials provided are insufficient. Subsequently, the coordinator that suggested workshops/TDPs be organised for their teachers, apart from using alternative pedagogic support, self-monitoring and teacher-support groups. However, he commented that the teachers do not use the Teacher Journal and Peer-Observation is not undertaken. The teachers do not have Teacher-Portfolios and do not employ the method of Team-Teaching and are less familiar with the knowledge of Case Analysis. The Coordinator concluded by saying that he is not satisfied with the training programme and suggested that the APSWREIS teachers be provided with all necessary materials to impart all the four skills. The teachers should be motivated to become committed and passionate. They should be appreciated for the work they do in schools and they should be made aware of the importance of English.

4.1. Semi-Structured Interview Transcripts of Resource Persons of Teacher Development Programmes at APSWREIS

Below are the responses of the resource persons to the questions of "How does the teacher development programme fulfill the objectives of APSWREIS in terms of giving appropriate inputs to the English language teachers? Almost all the resource persons were unaware of the objectives of the programme but it was mentioned by many of the resource persons that they were informed that the programme should cover two major components. The first component was the professional component. In this component the teachers were to be taught the techniques and strategies as to how they may teach vocabulary and grammar, improve speaking and writing skills, and develop appropriate reading strategies in the learners. The second component was related to improving the English language proficiency of the teachers themselves as they had some problems concerning with pronunciation and grammar. One resource person said that it was not good to predetermine objectives and needs beforehand. He visited the schools during a project the EFLU has undertaken and identified the needs but another resource person informed the researcher that he was not sure of the general objectives but when they were attended for the programme the resource persons designed the following objectives:

(a) To help teacher participants understand the important aspects while dealing with lessons in listening and speaking and help teacher participants experience, understand, and analyze a variety of listening and speaking activities; and

(b) To enable teacher participants to design lesson plans for [teaching] listening and speaking.

Most of the teachers in unequivocal voice said that they succeeded in giving those inputs, teaching various skills and language elements using interesting activities and communicative mode in addition to teaching methodology. The resource persons said that the participant teachers were satisfied with inputs given to large extent. One of the resource persons admitted that they failed in taking into consideration that the learners whom these teachers teach were first generation learners, parents mostly illiterates or very with low education; from low socio-economic status; coming to the school for the first time. He said that they taught in the teacher training programme as though it is the monolingual context. Another resource person said that they did not do needs analysis nor make an attempt to design the programme to suit the special needs of the teachers. In his opinion the programme met with their needs partially but they could do more.

4.2. Do these programmes incorporate the recent trends in ELT? If so, how? If not, why?

The resource persons Stated that participant teachers come with different baggage of experiences, imaginativeness, creativity, resourcefulness and they come with absolutely unique background in terms of economic background, family background and ability to understand things happening around them. They look at a particular phenomenon from their point of view and try to construct the knowledge of the world in a unique individualised manner. They stated that they demonstrated how these experiences and knowledge are exhibited in the class. They taught the "how" of teaching vocabulary and language skills in a holistic perspective and integrate them with other subjects. Resource persons gave some inputs regarding innovative practices. In the table given below there is a course outline for this programme:

Listening

Topic/ Activity in Focus	Theory and Reflection
Stories/Songs /Video (No overt responses)	Difference between listening in real life and listening in the English classroom Learner difficulties in Listening
Obeying instructions Ticking off items Detecting mistakes Guessing definitions (Short responses)	Approaches/Guidelines for the design of listening tasks Sub-skills of listening
Answering questions Note taking, Paraphrasing/Summarizing (Longer response)	Stages in a listening lesson/Steps in a listening lesson

Another resource person said, "I taught them the basics of evaluation, what is testing, what is content testing, what is language testing, how to make language items, how to write instructions, etc." Some resource persons said that they give the teachers an idea of text books that are prepared in line with the recent trends in language teaching and orient them to handle these text books using the latest techniques in the class rooms and connect them to the realities of the classroom situation, etc. A few resource persons taught task based teaching, authentic materials, how to make use of their experiences, exploiting cultural capital like: stories, songs from indigenous cultures. One of the strategies adopted in a sustained manner is to provide demonstration lessons, and also help the teachers develop appropriate lesson plans which they can use once they get back to school. Besides, they fostered positive learning by conducting learning activities based on audio material, helped them record some of the good language topics which they find on any media radio, TV, Internet sources. Resource persons have also given them some websites, where they can download authentic material, like BBC.com, Voice of America special English, YouTube as much as possible use it in the classrooms to give exposure to authentic English spoken by the native speakers as well as those who learn English as native speakers still can use neutral English which is intelligible to everybody.

Speaking

Topic/ Activity in Focus	Theory and Reflection
Integrated skill Activities	Principles of CLT
Oral Fluency Activities	Stages of an activity Activity Recipes Designing a Lesson plan

Information Gap Activities	Characteristics of a Successful Speaking Activity Challenges of conducting a Speaking Activity
Role Play	Role of a teacher in a Speaking lesson
Discussion Activities	Methods of and Materials for Speaking
Topic Based and Task Based Activity	Dealing with Errors Criteria for Evaluating a Speaking Lesson
Activity based Grammar	Speaking Competence: Grammatical and discourse knowledge
Pronunciation games	Speaking Competence: Lexical and Phonological knowledge

4.3. What is your opinion about the approaches, methods and materials used in the school curriculum? Do you think the TD Programme helps generate awareness about critiquing the present curriculum?

One of the resource persons said that now you know every training programme has three main objectives. The major objectives are ASK. "A" stands for attitudes teachers and learners comes to the class with different attitudes. "S" stands for skills. We want to hone the pedagogical skills of the trainees. We have observed time and again that teachers teach the way they want to teach. We give demonstration to them regarding how they could teach vocabulary or literature. It helps them to understand the skill of teaching language and understand the process of learning a second language more closely.

The resource person said that they liked the communicative methodology of the teaching and task based teaching etc. but they fall back on the earlier practices especially the lecture method when they go back to their schools. Training programme has some impact but on very few those teachers, who are really motivated to do something different. One resource person said he taught them group method, group techniques, pair work and group work, and also he laid emphasis on project work. Some of the resource persons said that there was no critical analysis of present curriculum and some others said they were not sure of the school curriculum related to approaches, methods and materials in English. Some other resource persons said that the purpose of the workshops is to train the teachers, and to make it easier for them to deal with the existing curriculum. Another resource person said that practicing teacher hardly ever gets an occasion to look at the curriculum. Hence no special sessions on critiquing the curriculum are included in the training programme, for this is considered to be redundant. One of the resource persons said that the textbook doesn't have much scope for teaching listening and speaking skills in the absence of any audio material along with any textbook. That explains abundantly that the textbook is not prepared for teaching listening and speaking. They were able to critique it towards the end of the Programme because they knew that the teacher development programme concentrated mainly on listening and speaking and they looked at their own textbooks they found that there was no scope for these two skills in the textbook. They were also able to critique the textbooks that were not structured around the communicative activities, and mainly the textbooks were based on structural approach and matter was teacher centric and used grammar translation. Apart from the teachers' voice there was no scope in the textbook for any other means through which the learners could get to hear English.

4.4. Do the training sessions equip teachers to prepare materials independently?

One of the resource persons said that the most teachers are text dependent. They want to teach the text book from cover to cover. They do not want to go beyond the text book. There are reasons for this. For example, the teacher feels very comfortable; the text book gives him/her a sense of security, and the teacher does not want to take risk. He/she feels that if he/she goes out of the text and develops independent materials then he/she may go wrong. The resource person stated that the most teachers use the text book and they do not go beyond the text books and cartoons, songs, greeting cards, newspaper clippings and they use these materials authentic materials no cost. The resource persons show that greeting cards clips can be used how these are available.

Some resource persons gave them model materials like: a six-line story or a simplified version of news to replicate them but the teachers had excuses saying they did not have computer and printer at schools to replicate them. The teacher participants did not seem very inclined to prepare their own materials because of the over-presence of the textbooks. A few resource persons said that they taught them how to use supplementary materials, especially the practice materials that are available. The resource person stated that he did give these teachers an idea to look outside the text books for outside materials and bringing those materials to teach English and practice language use. So this is done with a view to taking the classroom knowledge to the outside world and bring in outside experience to the classroom to meet the demands of the world in terms of the English language; project work also is also here. The resource person stated that some resource persons visited the schools, talked with the teachers, showed them material, invited them here, tried developing materials and got their feedback. That was how we involved them. One of them said that these training programmes are a general mix of topics with less time to deal with various topics. It should be thematic. Had it been thematic we would have more time to spend on material development alone. Nevertheless, resource person stated that some sessions are allotted to do tasks which the teachers are supposed to design by themselves.

Another resource person said that the programme included a component on analysis of the textbook and they found out its weakness. Having done this, the teachers are also trained to overcome the weaknesses by developing supplementary exercises so that the textbook becomes more relevant to the learners. This is a modest beginning, the resource person stated that in his experience he has found that teachers enjoy these tasks and exercises as they find it most relevant to their work. As the learners come from a village we think of the agricultural implements and things like hatchet, plough, etc. The teacher has to do a lot home work and make a list of agricultural implements or also animals, birds that are seen in the background–cows, buffalos, sparrows, goats, dogs, donkeys, chickens etc., and use them. The resource person said that teachers can be asked to construct riddles and crossword puzzles for the students. Further, resource person stated that there is a difference between APSWRIES Schools located in a village and a city. Because the backgrounds are different the resources are different teachers need to keep in mind this and then adapt, change, teachers strategies, methods and approaches and techniques and materials and so on and so forth. One resource person questioned the capabilities and aptitude of an average school teacher. He said, besides knowledge of teacher education and ability, one needs to understand and appreciate material production before even formulating this query. “Do you imagine that any individual however academically inclined and proficient in a language can prepare materials independently after one week's training?"

4.5. What are your views about language evaluation in the APSWREIS Schools? How do the TD programmes focus on educating teachers on principles of evaluation?

One of the resource persons said that "evaluation" in general itself is a very backward thing in our country. "We resort to traditional evaluation practices. Mostly we use summative evaluation." The resource person stated that teachers' view would be to give the students a sense of achievement through their valuation. That is the real evaluation. Teachers would make aware of their students' good points also along with the points which are to be improved. That is not happening at the schools. Another resource person felt that he always believed that teachers should not test the ignorance of the learners; it should always try to test the knowledge of the learners. Evaluation should not be an end in itself but a starting point for both the teachers and learners. The APSWREIS had materials which tested only reading and writing. But there is no scope for testing, listening and speaking.

Some of the resource persons believed in continuous comprehensive evaluation. They felt that it is not a good idea to evaluate the competence and performance of the learner once a year and twice a year; at the end of the semester and at the end of the year. In fact, it is a good idea to evaluate and to assess the performance and the competence of the learner on a day to day basis. The resource person stated how it can be done. Resource person tells the teachers to maintain a diary and write the profile of the learner. These are the weaknesses and strengths of the learner that this particular learner is good at vocabulary, but not so good at grammar. And then give that learner a chance to improve over a period of time. "We show them how we can and how we should cover language skills like reading, writing, study skills like dictionary skills, note making, note taking, summarising, précis writing etc and also language elements like vocabulary grammar and pronunciation. But, there is no control; actually, whether they do it in the classroom or not." The resource person said that "We tell them that this has to be done, this should be done; but after going back to their school we do not know what they do. I hope that at least some teachers practice and implement continuous and comprehensive evaluation. Some of them even prepared materials for language evaluation."

Another resource person informed that teachers should monitor the students from day one to the end and not through test. The resource person sated that there is a little discussion on evaluation in TD programme, because resource persons were largely focusing on giving skills to the teachers. One of the resource persons said that they should not enforce the same evaluation method everywhere. So here the teacher has to use his discretion and experience, when it comes to evaluation of language. A few of the resource persons said there hadn't been too much focus on it. Some of them were unsure of the current method of evaluation. Another resource person said that the programmes had not focussed on this aspect so far. The evaluation is dictated by the SCERT and the schools are expected to follow the same norms. Hence no special efforts are put in this direction. The state provides model question papers, item types for use on tests and schedules for test etc. Fortunately, the teachers in Society schools had more freedom to use their own methods, materials and testing strategies. He found many teachers doing this on their own initiative, and the Society does not propose this as a need when they depute teachers for training. One resource person mentioned that as per his observation, the APSWREIS teachers spent significant amounts of time with learners during the study hours as well as during self-study periods that were monitored by the teachers. During these periods some teachers took the initiative of making the learners read books outside the syllabus, or work on grammar and vocabulary exercises outside the textbooks and write new paragraphs. However, such teachers were the exception than the norm, and their efforts had to be appreciated. Observing and studying the teaching of English in the APSWREIS was a complex area of study, said one of the respondents, and it was unclear whether the sessions at the TDPs included evaluation techniques or principles.

It has been found out, based on the responses of the resource persons that there is a mismatch, to a large extent, between the needs of the participant teachers of APSWREIS and the topics that are being dealt with by the resource persons. The unexpected point is that some of the resource persons did not know what the objectives of the programme are. In addition, there are a lot of inconsistent responses for the same question. To conclude, the most important and conspicuous points that emerge here are:

(a) The Society has not stated its specific objectives explicitly while sending the participant teachers. The blind and general approach to teacher development programmes, such as this, will not help anyone – neither the teachers nor the learners, who are at the core of the issue.

(b) There is huge wastage of Society's money, wastage of time and energy of both the participant teachers and resource persons.

4.6. Practicing English Teachers' Questionnaire (Opinion) (Close-ended)

This section analyses the data collected through the closed-ended Questionnaire and finds out whether the teacher development programmes meet the needs and expectations of the teachers. The questionnaire has questions on context, syllabus, methodology, materials, pedagogy, alternative pedagogical support and evaluation patterns that the teacher development programmes would deal with to improve the participant teachers teaching at APSWREIS.

4.6.1 Section 1: Context

There are five questions in this section. The questions in this section were intended to find out whether teacher development programmes:

(i) help practicing English teachers to understand that English language teaching takes the help of learner's culture;

(ii) help practicing English teachers to teach learners, who belong to scheduled castes, scheduled tribes and other marginalised sections of the society;

(iii) should be designed based on their language proficiency and subject-matter knowledge;

(iv) should introduce teachers to relevant new research outcomes in English language teaching; and

(v) would benefit teachers more, if it teaches ABOUT the English language.

Syllabus

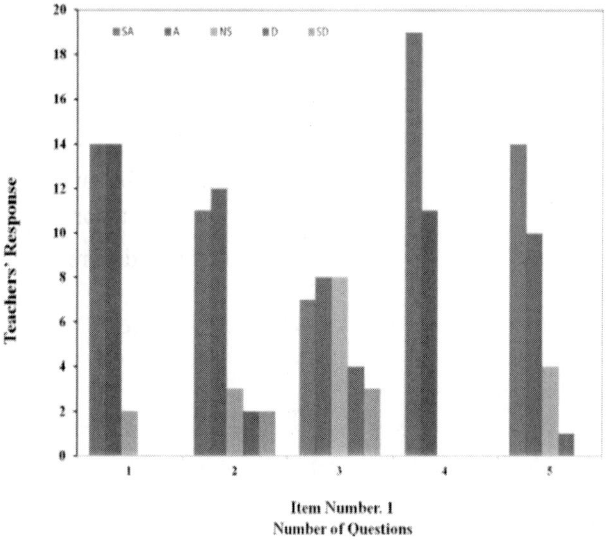

English Teachers' Response

	Q1	Q2	Q3	Q4	Q5
SA	14	11	7	19	14
A	14	12	8	11	10
NS	2	3	8	0	4
D	0	2	4	0	1
SD	0	2	3	0	0

SA: Strongly Agree

A: Agree;

NS: Not Sure;

D: Disagree;

SD: Strongly Disagree;

Q: Question

4.6.2. Figure and Table: Context

The above section on context has the following response. Among the respondent practicing English teachers, 80% of the teachers either strongly agreed or agreed for the items given above but 8% of them either strongly disagreed or disagreed. 11.3% of them were unsure.

4.6.3. Section 2: Syllabus

There are seven statements in this section. These items of the questionnaire were intended to find out practicing English teachers' opinion as to whether the teacher development programme:

(i) is only about the topics related to "how to teach" English to learners;

(ii) helps them to understand how English can be taught as a first, second or a foreign language and know their theories;

(iii) should also be about teaching learners with different talents and needs;

(iv) should have topics that guide them to think about their teaching;

(v) should guide them to teach English more effective by enquiring the learners;

(vi) should help them to connect English language teaching to life outside school; and

(vii) should make them think independently regarding the use of various methods, materials and evaluation in their English classrooms.

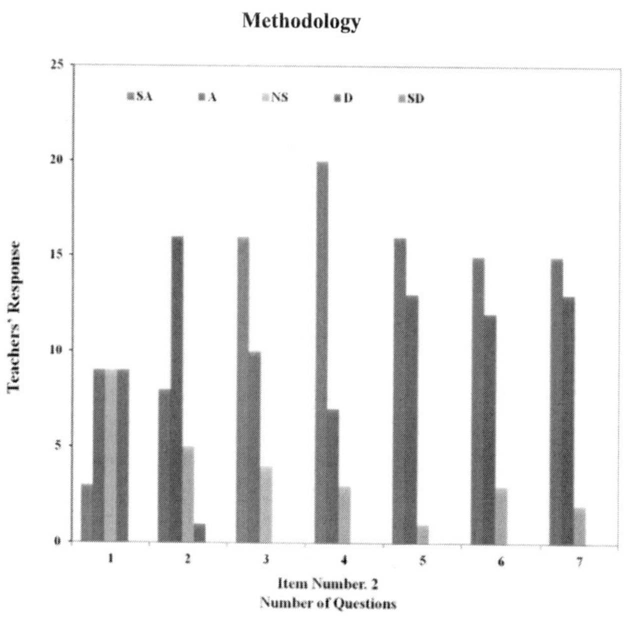

English Teachers' Response

	Q1	Q2	Q3	Q4	Q5	Q6	Q7
SA	3	8	16	20	16	15	15
A	9	16	10	7	13	12	13
NS	9	5	4	3	1	3	2
D	9	1	0	0	0	0	0
SD	0	0	0	0	0	0	0

SA: Strongly Agree
A: Agree
NA: Not Sure
D: Disagree
SD: Strongly Disagree
Q: Question

4.6.4. Figure and Table: Syllabus

It may be stated that the above section on syllabus has the following response. Among the respondent practicing English teachers, 82.3% of the teachers either strongly agreed or agreed but 4.7% of the teachers disagreed. However, 12.8% were unsure.

4.6.5. Section 3: Methodology

There are three questions in this section. The items of the questionnaire were intended to find out practicing English teachers' opinion as to whether the teacher development programmes should : (i) introduce them to a pool of method(s)/ approaches (es)/ eclecticism that may suit their future English classrooms, (ii) should make them analyze methods/ approaches critically and encourage them to use innovative ways of teaching English, and (iii) integrate English with the other subjects taught in the school, while teaching.

4.6.6. Figure and Table: Methodology

The above section on methodology has the following response from the practicing English teachers. 88.8% of the teachers either strongly agreed or agreed but 2.2% of them either disagreed or strongly disagreed for the third item only. However, 8.8% were unsure of their responses to the items given.

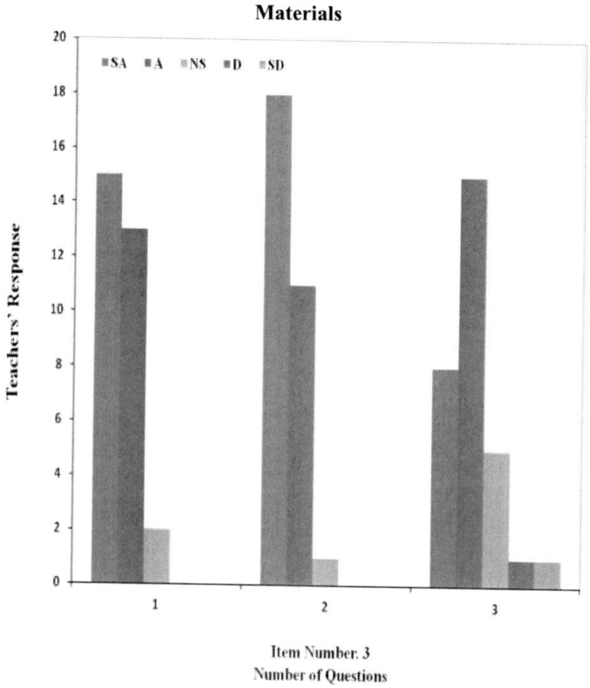

English Teachers' Response

	Q1	Q2	Q3
SA	15	18	8
A	13	11	15
NS	2	1	5
D	0	0	1
SD	0	0	1

SA: Strongly Agree
A: Agree
NA: Not Sure
D: Disagree
SD: Strongly Disagree
Q: Question

4.6.7. Section 4: Materials

There are three questions in this section. The items were intended to find out practicing English teachers' opinion as to whether the teacher development programmes should: (i) encourage them to read primary sources more, (ii) enable them to think independently and interact; and (iii) teach them with examples how to select and produce materials to teach English to different learners.

Materials

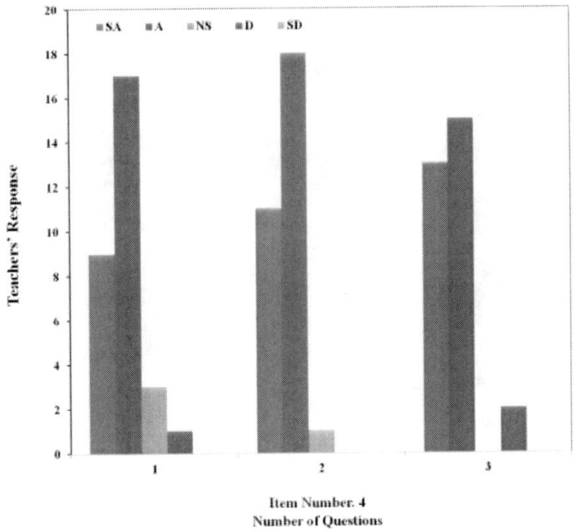

English Teachers' Response

	Q1	Q2	Q3
SA	9	11	13
A	17	18	15
NS	3	1	0
D	1	0	2
SD	0	0	0

SA: Strongly Agree
A: Agree
NA: Not Sure
D: Disagree
SD: Strongly Disagree
Q: Question

4.6.8. Figure and Table: Materials

The above section on methodology has the following response from the practicing English teachers. It was found among the respondent practicing English teachers, 92.2% of them either strongly agreed or agreed but 3.3% of them disagreed and 4.4% were unsure.

4.6.9. Section 5: Pedagogy

There are three questions in this section. The items of the questionnaire were intended to find out Practicing English Teachers' opinion whether the teacher development programmes: (i) must conduct video-recorded microteaching practice, (ii) conduct peer – teaching to evaluate their teaching skills and give them thorough feedback, and (iii) should expose them to multiple and diverse English language classrooms during the programme in view of globalisation.

Pedagogy

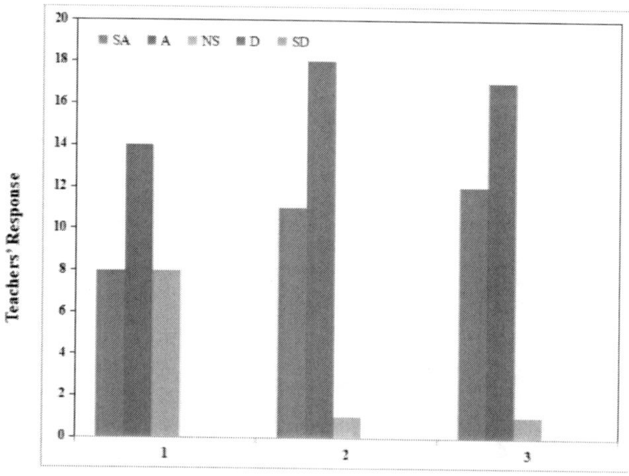

Item Number. 5
Number of Questions

English Teachers' Response

	Q1	Q2	Q3
SA	8	11	12
A	14	18	17
NS	8	1	1
D	0	0	0
SD	0	0	0

SA: Strongly Agree
A: Agree
NA: Not Sure
D: Disagree
SD: Strongly Disagree
Q: Question

4.3.5 Figure and Table: Pedagogy

The above section on Pedagogy has three questions. Among the respondent practicing English teachers, 88.8% either strongly agreed or agreed for all the three items. 11.1% were unsure and none disagreed to the statements given.

4.3.10. Section 6: Alternative Pedagogic Support

There are eight questions in this section. The items of the questionnaire were intended to find out Practicing English Teachers' opinion whether:

Alternative Pedagogic Support

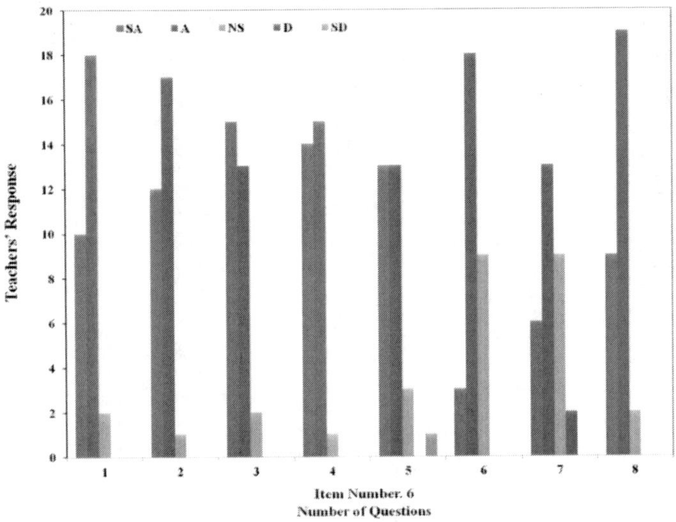

English Teachers' Response

	Q1	Q2	Q3	Q4	Q5	Q6	Q7	Q8
SA	10	12	15	14	13	3	6	9
A	18	17	13	15	13	18	13	19
NS	2	1	2	1	3	9	9	2
D	0	0	0	0	0	0	2	0
SD	0	0	0	0	1	0	0	0

SA: Strongly Agree
A: Agree
NA: Not Sure
D: Disagree
SD: Strongly Disagree
Q: Question

(i) they grasp better if workshops are conducted during teacher development programmes, (ii) self-monitoring improves their teaching, (iii) teacher –support groups enhance their pedagogical skills, (iv) teacher journal helps them to keep track of their improvement in teaching, (v) peer – observation of colleagues is valuable in knowing their errors in teaching, (v) teacher-portfolios are helpful to show their performance during a specific period of time, (vi) team – teaching enhances their teaching ability; and (viii) the knowledge of case analysis is important in assessing their teaching contexts.

4.3.11. Figure and Table: Alternative pedagogic support

The above section on alternative pedagogic support has eight questions. Among the respondent practicing English teachers, 85.2% of the teachers either strongly agreed or agreed to the items given, 0.4% strongly disagreed for the sixth item, 0.8% disagreed for the seventh item and 12 % were unsure.

4.3.12. Section 7: Evaluation

There is one question in this section. This item of the questionnaire was intended to find out practicing English teachers' opinion as to whether

Alternative Pedagogic Support

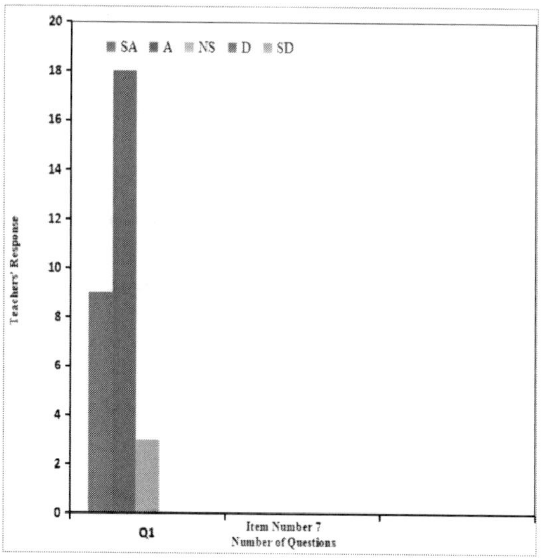

English Teachers' Response

	Q1
SA	9
A	18
NS	3
D	0
SD	0

SA: Strongly Agree
A: Agree
NA: Not Sure
D: Disagree
SD: Strongly Disagree
Q: Question

the teacher development programmes should introduce them learner friendly language evaluation like take-home tests, informal oral tests etc.

4.3.13. Figure and Table: Evaluation

Among the respondent practicing English teachers, 90% either strongly agreed or agreed, 10% were unsure, 0% disagreed or strongly disagreed to the statement given.

4.3.14. Section 8: Suggestions

There are four questions in this section. The items were intended to find out Practicing English Teachers' opinions on whether: (i) it would be helpful for them if action research is taught during the teacher development programmes, (ii) information related to library resources, journals, e-journals, should be given during TDPs, (iii) membership in professional bodies and paper presentations could update their knowledge related to teaching and (iv) international teacher exchange programmes with English – Speaking countries would help them gain important inputs related to theory and practical aspects.

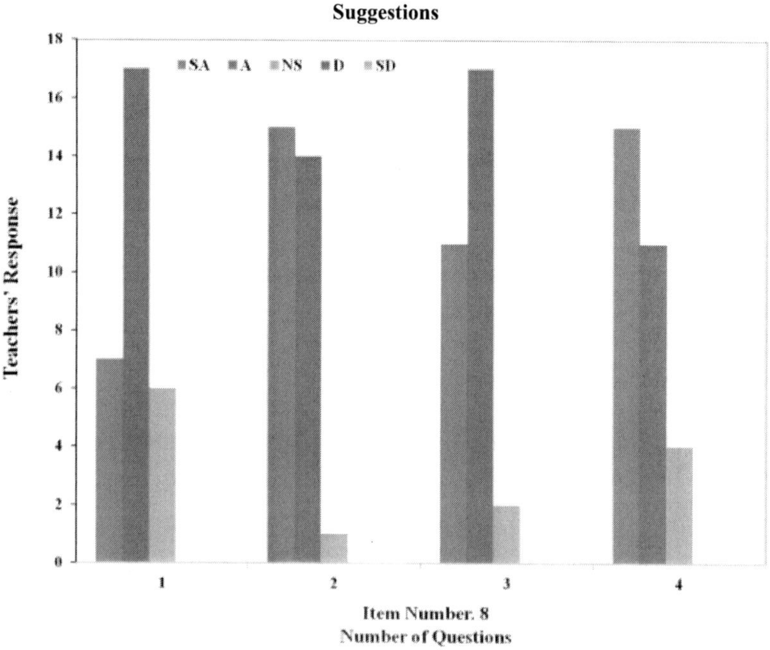

English Teachers' Response

	Q1	Q2	Q3	Q4
SA	7	15	11	15
A	17	14	17	11
NS	6	1	2	4
D	0	0	0	0
SD	0	0	0	0

SA: Strongly Agree
A: Agree
NA: Not Sure
D: Disagree
SD: Strongly Disagree
Q: Question

4.3.15. Figure and Table: Suggestions

Among the respondent practicing English teachers, 89.3% of them either strongly agreed or agreed, 10.6 % were unsure and none of them strongly disagreed or at least disagreed to the statements given. It is observed that 87.07% of the respondents have either strongly agreed or agreed to the statements given. Only mere 8% respondents have either disagreed or strongly disagreed to the statements given above. Interestingly, there was no disagreement on the items related to "pedagogy", "evaluation" and "suggestions". 10.12% respondents were unsure of their responses. They neither agreed nor disagreed on the items given above. Based on the above findings a conclusion can be drawn that eighty seven percent respondents agreed to the items given above. As 10.12% of respondents do not disagree with the statements, we can assume that they too form a part of the group of respondents whose response was "agree". It also implies that most of the teachers believe that changes should take place based on the opinions expressed given above. In general, the teachers have a good awareness of what is required in TDPs and by implication what is required of them as teachers.

4.7. Analysis of Practicing English Teachers' Questionnaire (Open Ended)

Finally, around 30 teachers were asked to comment on the TDPs that they had attended and on the strategies of teaching related aspects. However, the responses of 10 teachers have been taken for the present study. These respondents are the in-service teachers working at the selected schools administered by the APSWREIS. They were asked to comment on the following aspects, viz., the social and cultural background of the students; issues relating to the overall curriculum and syllabus content; the appropriacy of the materials being used and scope for training in independent materials production; approaches and methods of teaching English; evaluation; teacher beliefs and learner beliefs; action research; research awareness.

4.8. The social and cultural background of the students

Are these contexts discussed in these programmes? Are teachers sensitised to these contexts?

8 out of 10 teachers have responded that the TDPs have discussed and sensitized them about the socio-cultural aspects of the students.

Do you believe that inputs would have a bearing on your classroom teaching? How?

8 out of 10 teachers have responded that the inputs of the social and their cultural background of the students discussed at the TDPs would have a bearing on classroom teaching.

Do you believe that sensitisation of this kind is required in future programmes? Why?

All the 10 teachers have responded that they strongly do believe about the requirement in the future TDPs for the sensitisation of teachers to social and cultural background of the students.

What measures do you employ to take the students' background into account?

9 out of 10 teachers – discussed about the measures that they employ to take the students' background into account, viz., a base line test can be conducted; an easily understandable questionnaire can be provided to the students; passing information to the students and encouraging them to take interest; motivating; educational social background; by knowing the students family history; the festivals they celebrate; the region they belong to and so on. Following this, the other measures employed were by speaking to them personally; speaking to their parents; by giving any particular work to know about them and their background; by enquiring about their family; educational background; entertain them to speak in English; write short stories; E-plus activities will be done and so on. However, in the regular teaching practice it was found that a very few were employing the above-mentioned measures – this practice existed only with a very few teachers' regular practice as a classroom observation. Therefore, it may be stated that the above section on social and cultural background of the students has four questions posing about aspects related to discussion and contextualisation of socio-cultural background of students, sensitisation of the above mentioned at the TDPs and requirements for future programmes, assumptions that the inputs if gained would have a bearing on the participants classroom teaching, measures employed by the teacher to take the students' background into account in the overall Open Ended Questionnaire. Among the respondent Practicing English Teachers, 80% have agreed that they are sensitized about the socio-cultural background of students, while 20% were not sure and did not properly respond to the questions asked by researcher.

4.9. Issues relating to the overall curriculum and syllabus content

Which aspects of curriculum, syllabus and materials production are discussed in these programmes?

9 out of 10 teachers responded and agreed that there was a discussion regarding the aspects of curriculum, syllabus and materials production. They were mainly about teaching techniques; effective use of teaching aids; making classroom teaching more effective; presentation-practice-production; describing things; Grammar; Verbs and so on. The Grammar part was conducted mainly through the usage of several examples. They responded that the Curriculum, Syllabus and materials issued by the Government and Communicative aspects of Curriculum, tasks with clear objectives were discussed. But, in the observation of the researcher it was found that the above-mentioned aspects are totally ignored in the respondents' regular practice – in the classroom observation.

4.10. How do these discussions aid your classroom teaching?

Nine out of ten teachers' response to the question: 'How the discussions of curriculum, syllabus and materials production have aided their classroom teaching,' disclosed that the classroom teaching can be made more effective through the discussions at the TDPs. They have aided the respondent in helping the students, enrich his/her classroom teaching. Some of the lessons, viz., "Robots and People", "Eight Cousins or One Brother" have given the teacher scientific knowledge, other lessons have made them feel happy and relaxed after imparting them to the student. The sessions at the TDPs have facilitated the respondents in making their students understand the content easily. They remarked that the discussions have assisted them in making the children understand the content easily, mostly in a play way. Some of the discussions at the TDP sessions were brought up as instances in the classroom – so as to make the pupils realise their goals and strength. Some respondents have stated that the TDPs have assisted them in preparing activities, which are relevant to any children. The discussions have enabled the respondents with a deeper understanding of the text; give more illustrations to explain the context clearly. However, in the researcher's observance – in the classroom observation, it has been identified that most of the above mentioned aspects were totally ignored in the respondents' regular practice.

4.11. Do you prepare any supplementary materials for your classes? If so, give details and explain why?

All the 10 teachers have responded to the question: 'Do you prepare any supplementary materials for your classes? If so, give details and explain why'. A summary is drawn below based on the teachers' response: They responded that they employ charts for teaching structural items and do concentrate much on A.V. Aids, Skits, etc. as these materials are regarded by the respondents would create interest among the students to learn. However, in the researcher's observance – in the classroom observation, it has been identified that largely the respondents have ignored scrap books and oral exercises to teach the language interestingly. Sentence flip cards, flash cards, puzzles, etc. were not utilised to make the learners understand better. Many teaching aids like Newspapers, wedding cards, greeting cards, tourist guides, railway timetable etc. were not employed to improve the communicative skills of their learners.

4.12. Do you think more of discussions on these topics are required in future programmes? Why?

All the 10 practicing English language teachers mentioned that more discussions were required in future programmes.

Conclusion: To conclude, it may be stated that the above section on issues relating to the overall curriculum and syllabus content has four questions about aspects related to aspects of curriculum, syllabus and materials production, discussions aiding their classroom teaching, preparation of any supplementary material for their classes and need for more discussions on curriculum and syllabus content required in future TDPs in the overall Open Ended Questionnaire. Among the respondent Practicing English Teachers, 90% have agreed that there was a discussion on curriculum, syllabus and materials production. They have further noted that the above discussions were aiding their classroom teaching. They mentioned that they do prepare supplementary materials for their classroom. Moreover, they said that they require discussions on these topics for future programmes. However, 10% were not sure and did not properly respond to the questions asked by researcher

4.13. The appropriacy of materials used and scope for training in independent materials production.

What do you think about the level of language used in the text?

There were 9 teachers who responded to the question: 'What do they think about the level of language used in the text?' by opining that the level of language is apt to the standard of students; it would be more helpful if it is made simpler. They noted that it was good, simple and comprehensible. Furthermore, responded that it was appropriate. Some of the respondents mentioned that the language in the text was simple and can be easily comprehended by the learners. However, in some lessons, the respondents mentioned that too many words were used, as this would decrease the learners' interest of self-reading.

How are the materials culturally appropriate to the learners?

Out of 10 teachers 9 responded that materials portray local cultural factors that are very much familiar to the children. Hence, they seem culturally appropriate to the leaners. The respondents mentioned that some themes, nature, cultural background employed in the materials are already recognizable to the children. The materials are very much useful to the learners as they inform about live situations, experiences and look natural. However, one respondent said that the materials are not culturally appropriate to the learners and did not elaborate on the remark.

How do the materials respond to the social issues of the learners?

Out of 10 teachers 8 responded to the question that the materials make the leaners realise their responsibility of growing up and reaching to a good status in the society. The Audio material, visual material, the prescribed textbooks are considered by them to be authentic material. They responded that the material gives ample space to reflect on the attitudes of the students. They are able to connect the material with their personal life and it is making the learners to remember their social background and culture. The learners can relate the text to their real-life situations.

How often do the Teacher Development Programmes provide any training to independently create new material or adapt existing material?

Out of 10 teachers 9 responded that the TDPs provide training to independently create new material or adapt existing material regularly. The time frame that the respondents have mentioned approximately may be said is undertaken once in every three months. They comprise of issues, viz., describing things, guessing games, filled word puzzles and so on. The respondents mentioned that they are able to create and adapt existing material. Furthermore, the TDPs, mentioned by the respondents, provide opportunities and assist them to approach the textbook in a different way to create new material.

Therefore, it may be stated that the above section on the appropriacy of the materials being used and scope for training in independent material production contains four questions about aspects related to level of language used in the text, whether materials are culturally appropriate to the learners, whether materials correspond with social issues of the learners and how often the TDP's provide training for independent creation of new materials or adapt existing materials in the overall Open Ended Questionnaire. Among the respondent Practicing English Teachers, 90% have agreed that the level of language used in the text was apt to suit the standard of the learners, and the materials delivered to the student were culturally appropriate. They opined that the materials do respond to the social issues of the learners. Finally, they responded that the TDPs do provide opportunities and assist them to approach the textbook in a different way to create new material. However, 10% were not sure and did not properly respond to the questions asked by researcher.

4.14. Approaches and Methods of Teaching English

Do the TD programmes raise your awareness with regard to approaches and methods? What training do they provide in traditional and alternative approaches and methods?

Out of 10 teachers 8 teachers responded that the TDPs raise awareness as well as polish the already learnt approaches and methods. Furthermore, the respondents described the TDPs do provide training to use suitable approach to the apt situations. They have raised awareness – discrete testing the respondents integrates testing. It refers to testing only skill - sub-skill and skill. They have opined that the traditional methods of training prove to be a mere waste and everything should be taught in a practical way in these days. However, the rest of respondents have mentioned that no sufficient trainings are provided.

How has such training, if any, helped in your own classroom situation?

All the 10 teachers have responded that the training has brought innovation in their teaching style which made pupils enthusiastic and classroom teaching effective. Furthermore, the training has made the subject easy and classroom teaching has become a very easy task. It has made the classroom student centered. The TDPs are regarded by the respondents to have remarkably assisted in classroom teaching;

especially grammar teaching. The children have been exposed to creative activities. The respondents, in addition, opined that self-learning has brought an outburst in the students' learning skills. The training of dealing with CCE texts has helped a lot when they had tried it out in their class. The respondents' students were able to frame many sentences on their own when the cover picture was exploited. Consequently, the EGMM training is mentioned by the respondents as having helped them in teaching grammar by involving all the students in activities. However, in the researcher's observance – classroom observation, most of the above mentioned opinions were largely neglected in the teacher's regular practice.

Do you try out different methods of teaching for the following aspects: Listening, Speaking, Reading, Writing, Vocabulary, Grammar, Study Skills

All the 10 teachers responded that they do try out different methods of teaching aspects, viz., Listening, Speaking, Reading, Writing, Vocabulary, Grammar, Study skills. However, in the researcher's observance – classroom observation, all these aspects of teaching fail to be observed in the respondents' regular practice.

Do you think the future teacher development programmes should have more of this kind of training in Methodology and Teaching Aids?

All the 10 teachers opined that the future TDPs should have more of this kind of training in Methodology and Teaching Aids.

Hence, it may be stated that the above section on approaches and methods of teaching English has four questions about aspects related to TDPs raising awareness with regard to approaches and methods, the training provided through traditional and alternative approaches and methods, training to aid the participants' classroom situation, the different methods of teaching tried out, with reference to (listening, speaking, reading, writing, vocabulary, grammar, study skills), and whether the future TDP's have more of this kind of training in methodology and teaching aids in the overall Open Ended Questionnaire. Among the respondent Practicing English Teachers, 80% have agreed that the TDP's have raised awareness with regard to approaches and methods of teaching English and TDP's have provided training in discrete testing of the respondents, integrates testing related to testing only skill - sub-skill and skill. They have opined that the traditional methods of training, proves to be a mere waste of time and energy recommended adopting a practical methodology. Moreover, they responded that they do try out various methods for teaching listening, speaking, vocabulary, study skills and grammar. Furthermore, the opined that the future TDP's should have more of this kind of training in methodology and teaching aids. However, 10% were not sure and did not properly respond to the questions asked by researcher.

4.15. Evaluation

Do the TD programmes discuss evaluation practices and train you to evaluate more appropriately? If so, which aspects?

All the 10 teachers responded that the TDPs discuss evaluation practices and train them to evaluate more appropriately, viz., Formative – summative; listening; speaking; reading and writing skills; in correcting notes; Vocabulary; paragraph comprehension; teaching and interaction Furthermore, they have opined that the TDPs discuss evaluation practices and give ideas of observation and various methods. In addition, some sessions comprised of the topic: taking feedbacks for every activity reflection on teaching and learning. However, in the researcher's observance – classroom observation, the above mentioned evaluation practices were failed to be observed in the respondents' regular practice.

What effect do these programmes have on your classroom practices?

Out of 10 respondents 9 responded that the TDPs have an effect on classroom practice such as: They add some more grace to the respondents' teaching practices. It will bring in the child an overall development. The future learners can be assisted and suitable teaching method may be evolved. Learners feel ease to understand the language. The programmes bring effectiveness, lot of interaction and imbibe a natural way of learning every day. The TDPs are considered by the respondents as effective in improving the teaching learning practices. However, in the researcher's observance – classroom observation, the effect of TDPs has hardly had an effect in their regular practice.

What methods and measures of evaluation do you practice in your teaching?

All the 10 teachers responded by mentioning their methods and measures of their evaluation that they practice in their classroom teaching such as: Questioning; making students retell what is told by the teacher; Bilingual method; grammar translation; deductive fluency and accuracy. The respondents further mentioned that they practice evaluation methods, viz., slip test; oral test; oral tests; slip tests; unit tests, dictation, elocutions, and so on. Subsequently, they opined that they implement practices, viz., discussion; Learner centered method; Bilingual method; interactions; enacting; making the pupils reteach what they understand; by asking the questions; comprehension; questions; oral and written tests constructed and conducted for the learners. However, in the researcher's observance – classroom observation, it is observed that a very few methods and measures were found to be practiced in their regular teaching.

Do you think the future teacher development programmes should have more discussion on evaluation beliefs and practices? Why?

Out of 10 respondents 9 mentioned that the future teacher development programmes should have more discussion on evaluation beliefs and practices because, what a child learns is more important than what is taught in the class. It is concerned giving a critical judgment about the relation between aims and objectives. In addition, the respondents have mentioned that the aspect of Skill practice performed more in the classroom would develop an individual nature in the students. Moreover, an effective T.L. process – to bring forth the overall development in a child and to prepare the teacher into an expert in the evaluation of the children – is considered as important by the respondents.

Therefore, it may be stated that the above section on Evaluation has four questions about aspects related to TDPs discussing evaluation practices and training the participants to evaluate more appropriately, effect of TDPs on the participants' classroom practices, methods and measures of evaluation practised by the participants while teaching, and need for discussions on evaluation beliefs and practices in future TDPs in the overall Open Ended Questionnaire. Among the respondent Practicing English Teachers, 90% of the responses affirmed that the TDP's discuss evaluation practices and train the participants to evaluate more appropriately by taking feedbacks for every activity and involves reflecting on teaching and learning. However, the participants did not respond, when questioned on the particularity of the evaluation practices. Further, they responded that the sessions on evaluation at the TDPs have assisted in bringing an overall development in their classroom. The respondents, in addition, mentioned that the activities they organised in their classroom involved questioning; encouraging students to recaptivate or summarise what has been taught by the teacher; Bilingual method; grammar translation method; deductive fluency and accuracy. Subsequently, they opined that the future TDPs should have more discussions on evaluation beliefs and practices. However, 10% were not sure and did not properly respond to the questions asked by researcher.

4.16. Teacher Beliefs and Learner Beliefs

Do the TDPs focus on topics like teacher beliefs and learner beliefs?

Out of 10 teachers 8 have expressed their consent that the TDPs focus on topics like teacher beliefs and learner beliefs.

Have these discussions made a difference to your teaching practices in the classroom.

Out of 10 teachers 9 responded that these discussions made a difference to teaching practices in the classroom.

Are you aware of these concepts independently of training programmes? Do they have any bearing on your teaching? If so how?

Out of 10 teachers 7 aware of these concepts independently of training programmes. No teacher was responded properly to the later part of the question.

Do you think the future TD programmes should have more of such discussions?

All the 10 teachers mentioned that the future TD programmes should have more of such discussions.

Therefore, it may be stated that the above section on Teacher Beliefs and Learner Beliefs contains four questions about aspects related to TDPs focusing on topics like teacher beliefs and learner beliefs, discussions reasoning in bringing a difference in the participants' teaching practices in real classroom situation, whether the respondents were aware of these concepts independent of TDPs and their bearing on their teaching and the need for discussions on teacher beliefs and learner beliefs in future TDPs in the overall Open Ended Questionnaire. Among the respondent Practicing English Teachers, 70% have given their responses that the TDP's focus on topics like teacher beliefs and learner beliefs. They mentioned that the discussions do bring differences in their teaching practices in their real-time classroom situation. Moreover, 70% were aware of these concepts independently of training programmes. But, no participant responded properly to the later part of the question. Subsequently, they opined that the future TDPs should have more discussions on teacher beliefs and learner beliefs. However, 30% were not sure and did not properly respond to the questions asked by researcher.

4.17. Action research

How do TD programmes help and guide you in developing research projects, especially in relation to your teaching context?

Out of 10 teachers 7 responded that TDPs help and guide them in developing research projects, especially in relation to the teaching context.

Have you been able to take any of these issues to the classrooms for experiment or discussion? If yes, give an example.

Out of 10 teachers 8 responded that they are able to take any of these issues to the classrooms for experiment or discussion, such as enactment of traffic in class VII while teaching the poem, "A Town Boy". Furthermore, they opined that they have taught using TV/computer/gadgets etc. and implemented practice sessions among pupils by making them to teach what they listened and understood.

Have you implemented any research projects in your teaching? If yes, give an example.

Out of 10 teachers 5 responded and mentioned that they implemented research projects in their teaching, but failed to give examples.

What is your opinion about having such discussions in future teacher development programmes?

Out of 10 teachers 8 responded by opining that the TDPs have assisted in building up a healthy environment in the classroom and such discussions were further required in future teacher development programmes. They have responded that having such discussions in the TDPs improves one's personality and an all-around development. In addition, they have responded that the aspect of research helps teachers to study the students deeply and teaching becomes insightful. It promotes knowledge, new methods to handle and teaching English language. They reduce the burden of teachers and the student's role - learning methods. They remarked that more programmes should be conducted to update teacher's skills. There should more of enriching programmes to refresh their ideas, teaching learning methods. Therefore, it may be stated that the above section on Action Research has four questions about aspects related to TDPs helping and guiding in developing research projects in relation to their teaching context, the participants ability to research in classroom for experimentation or discussions, implementation of research projects in teaching, opinion about such discussions in future TDPs in the overall Open Ended Questionnaire. Among the respondent Practicing English Teachers, 60% responded that with positivity that TDP's do guide and help in developing research projects. They conferred that they do research in classroom and experimented and implemented research projects while teaching, but failed to give examples. Subsequently, they opined that the future TDPs should have more discussions on Action Research. However, 40% were not sure and did not properly respond to the questions asked by researcher.

4.18. Research awareness

Do these programmes help and guide you in accessing library resources, journals and e-journals, become members in Professional Bodies, make Paper Presentations and enable you to develop you as insightful teacher?

Out of 10 teachers 8 responded stating that these programmes help and guide them in accessing library resources, journals and e-journals, become members in Professional Bodies, make Paper Presentations and enable them to develop them as insightful teacher.

Do such reading and activities help you in your classroom teaching?

Out of 10 teachers 9 responded by mentioning that such reading and activities help them in classroom teaching.

Has your classroom interaction led you to think of research? If yes, give details.

Out of 10 respondents 4 remarked that classroom interaction led them to think of research but failed to give proper details.

Do you think future TD programmes should provide more of such information and discussion?

All the 10 teachers mentioned that the future TD programmes should provide more of such information and discussion.

Therefore, it may be stated that the above section on Research Awareness contains four questions about aspects related to TDPs helping and guiding in accessing library resources, journals and e-journals, to become members of professional bodies, paper presentations evolve as an insightful teacher, engaging reading, organising activities to help the participants, classroom interaction, promotion of research, and finally, providing information and encouraging discussion on research awareness - provided in future TDPs in the overall Open Ended Questionnaire. Among the respondent Practicing English Teachers, 60% responded that the TDP's guide and help in accessing library resources, journals and e-journals, become members of Professional Bodies, aid Paper Presentations and enable them to develop as an insightful teacher. They responded that reading activities help them in classroom teaching. They further remarked that classroom interaction encouraged them to engage in research but failed to provide proper details. Subsequently, they opined that the future TDPs should have more discussions on Research awareness. However, 40% were not sure and did not properly respond to the questions asked by researcher.

4.19. Teacher Development Programmes

The programmes attended by the researcher are the following:

S. No.	Title of the Programme	Univ./Instt.	Place
	Teacher Enrichment Programme	EFLU	Hyderabad
	Oral Communication Skills	EFLU	Hyderabad
	Communication Skills	EFLU	Hyderabad
	Reading Wise Programme	Purn Foundation	Hyderabad

APSWREIS Teacher Enrichment Programme

It has been suggested by one of the Resource persons that the teachers have to think from the learners' point of view. The participants are to play the role of learner in the in-service teacher enrichment programme. The programme aimed at addressing teaching methods and teaching materials etc.; furthermore, it was mentioned that teacher attitudes towards learners ought not to be - teacher centered and teacher dominated. Teacher has to motivate learners and act as a facilitator. He also agreed that no one method was the best method in the English language classroom. But, the teacher can go for composite methods. Every teacher has to update his/her knowledge towards new methodology and strategies. He added that even though there are equivalent words in the mother tongue, teachers were not using them in the classrooms; he emphasized the use of mother tongue in English language classrooms. One of the resource persons was affiliated directly to APSWREIS head office. He was deputed as a resource person for science as a mentoring teacher. He delivered a talk on problems faced by the teachers in the English language classroom, especially with first generation learners. He appealed to the trainers in the field of ELT to give more insights to develop and solve these problems to give better education to society. The researcher observed that the component "Teaching writing" was a major topic at the TDPs. There were issues raised by trainers relating to the process or product writing as it takes a lot of changes, many drafts are to be written at the process stage (re-writing, revising and editing) before the product is given a final shape. One of the resource person was heard asking the teachers: "How do you teach writing?" To this, some of the teachers responded by hinting at their roles as teachers and their job profile.

Many of them ended up teaching alphabets, and spellings. They did not think from the students' point of view. The trainer stressed the need to come down to the level of students so that the student would understand the processes involved in writing. He further suggested possible ways to go about teaching writing effectively. One aspect that the researcher faced in a discussion at the TDPs was Teaching Connectors. At this point, one of the Resource persons gave a story to teach connectors to the participants. Once the story was narrated in the classroom, the trainer asked the teachers the difference between speech/writing. He explained the differences in detail.

The other important component that was discussed at the TDPs was Methods of Teaching. The resource person introduced himself and he asked the participants' background, and such details. After that, he concentrated on students' needs and socio-economical and cultural background. He then zeroed in on importance of the English language for first generation learners. He claimed he had motivated and inspired several students to learn English. He asked questions and answers to interact with teachers. He asked questions like: How they felt about their classes? This class is an excellent class, when do you feel extremely happy? Are you satisfied with the class? Did you feel today I've done a good job in teaching? He asked the teachers to find some reasons like: Reasons why I think my class was highly successful/satisfying (a) well prepared (b) class is interactive, delighted (c) go beyond (d) feedback own/learners. Some of them had done extremely well. He addressed an existential question: "Why did I fail as teacher in the class" and asked for solutions. The trainer stressed the need to use multimedia- Internet, (electronic media) teaching aids, extending teaching ability to teach well. He further stressed, "Method is in your mind" and gave a few examples of Inductive method, Deductive method, Bilingual method, audio-lingual method so on and so forth.

Learner friendly method: Learner friendly methods were taught and a few suggestions were given: "Please treat students as your own children. You know, how your child thinks, what are their needs? What is best for your students? Create your own methodology; you are a learner/teacher, what are the problems you have? Make a list of problems? What are the negative aspects in you? Where did you fail? How? What are other reasons? Really you have to motivate them. Give more aspiration about their life. Teacher is a model for them. Reasons for failure:

Lessons can be problematic/difficult,

Lack of preparation (circumstantial),

Unable (inability) to cope with syllabus coverage,

Translation method,

Positive attitude brings about thoughts like: "Can I change my methodology? Won't make it habit of translation, Adaptation of methodology, "De-solve", More preparation, Group work/pair work. Your children are imaginative and creative, teaching a lesson- teaching how to learn, outside the classroom, inside the classroom."

Teaching Grammar: Brainstorming: "what do you mean by grammar? Principles of language usage, trainer interacts with trainees for few minutes. Exploring ideas, thoughts relating to teaching English grammar at school level. Grammar is principles of language usage. Rules of syntax sentence construction, group of words makes sentence, usage in situation. Lack of rules in grammar, lack of vocabulary relatively unknowing a word category or like grammatical category. How we can use the same word as a noun, verb, adj., and Adverb etc. while learning vocabulary we also concentrate on word grammatical category. Grammar teaching if you enjoy yourself by teaching/learning. Teaching enjoy fully otherwise it is monotonous, boring. How do I create an interest in the class? How do I help them internalise grammar point? Are you supplementing materials? Guessing / interpretation so and on so. There is no relation between time & tense."

	Time		
Experience	sex	number	meaning
	Tense		
Grammatical Category	gender	number	form

If he asked me, I would refuse- hypothetical

The PM flies to USA next week	- future
I go to the library everyday	- habitual
Did you come here to consult me	- time past – tense present
If he comes tell me	- future

Trainees are being taught tenses, passive voice, and prepositions

All of these tasks used with activities. The teachers enjoyed doing them in the class. But they were not interested in doing home work.

Teaching Vocabulary: Word games, leaflets, word mapping, concept mapping, and matching exercises. Lack of communication skills, more important to spoken English. Teachers have pessimistic notions about teaching vocabulary. Main goal is familiarising the words, as many words as possible. Teacher Trainer has given an assignment on developing a simple task to teach vocabulary. Teachers come up with their own vocabulary tasks using the hand out given by Trainer.

(a) form a word (tree with subject)
(b) matching the following word with suitable opposites
(c) put the following jumbled letters in order
(d) arrange the following words correct heading
(e) supply the missing letters
(f) make the words with –ing form, etc.

Teaching Listening, Teaching spoken English, understanding communication: Teaching listening has given importance to the purpose of listening, and how to teach listening. The lecture on teaching spoken English lecture was on teaching attitudes, mother tongue influence, and habit formation. In short, the programme was innovative and useful to all teachers of ELT. It was an eye opener to know the multifaceted nature of language teaching as a whole. Such programmes should be conducted frequently to help teachers improve their teaching potential. One of the TDPs at a training institute had classes entitled "Teacher Enrichment Programme Modules: Theory and Reflection." These classes concentrated mainly on the components, viz., reflective teaching and action research. APSWREIS teachers were taken gradually through the process of reflective teaching. The teachers were taught to have listening and speaking skills designed and instructed through particular models (difference between listening in real life and listening in the English classroom, sub-skills of listening, practice, stages in a listening lesson, principles of CLT, methods and materials of speaking) and to correlate with their teaching material to make certain whether they succeeded in their objectives or not.

The teachers were instructed to reflect upon the approaches/ guidelines for the design of listening tasks and speaking. In reference to action research, the teachers were asked to explicate the problems of conducting a speaking activity and design a plan of action as to how to address specific classroom issues. One TDP at EFLU had classes entitled "Teacher Development Programme Modules: Communication Skills." In this development programme the teachers were taught to enhance the speaking and reading skills of students using interactive mode. The Resource person taught the teachers on how to make students use visual images. The teachers were further asked to do pre-reading activities. These activities were regarded as supporting teachers in real time classroom teaching students about comprehension. The classes focused on the significance of experiential and constructivist techniques in the teaching of reading and speaking, where teachers were expected to tap into the background knowledge of students and offer student-centered activities to promote communication abilities. Most of the Resource persons dealt with the significance of a range of instructional methodologies employed to move students gradually towards a better understanding and, in the long run, more objectivity in the learning procedures. The Resource persons counselled the participants on how a teacher should lead students through challenging readings to reduce nervousness that regularly goes along with English language teaching.

4.20. Oral Communication Skills and Communication Skills

One session: Stories/Songs/Video, RPs explained the difference between listening in real life and listening in the English classroom.

Learner difficulties in Listening; Two sessions on Obeying instructions, detecting mistakes, guessing meaning and definitions from the context (Short responses) and approaches/Guidelines for the design of listening tasks, Sub-skills of listening to the participants. Another session answering questions, Note taking, Paraphrasing/Summarising keeping some of study skills (Longer response); Stages in a listening lesson/Steps in a listening lesson. These activties focused on Listening and speaking narration of stories, Listening songs and watching videos, etc. The Two sessions dedicated for Integrated skill on oral fluency Activities using Principles of Communicative Language Teaching introduced to the teachers, how to employ Stages of an activity (3 Ps presentation -practice-produce) Activity Recipes, Designing a Lesson plan. Two sessions to teach Information Gap Activities, Characteristics of a Successful Speaking Activity, Challenges of conducting a Speaking Activity to contextualising learner situation.

Teachers were given inputs on the following activities, Role Play: Role of a teacher in a Speaking lesson; Discussion Activities: Methods and Materials for Speaking; Topic Based and Task Based Activity: Dealing with Errors Criteria for Evaluating a Speaking Lesson

Activity based Grammar: Speaking Competence: Grammatical and discourse knowledge; Pronunciation games: Speaking Competence: Lexical and Phonological knowledge, etc.

4.21. Teacher Development Programme: "Reading Wise Programme."

One other programme at the Andhra Pradesh Academy of Rural Development (APARD) had classes entitled "Teacher Development Programme Modules: Reading Wise Programme." The classes dealt with reading instruction methods. In these classes, the participants were introduced to several kinds of reading and some of the factors were in tune with teaching methods. The teachers were briefed about the philosophy of new text books, viz., the basic principles based on which the text books were developed; Subject specific academic standards/ competencies or attainment targets were recommended in the text books and for the teaching learning process; Planning – Annual and unit-cum-lesson plans; Demonstration of Model lessons focusing on the steps for teaching; People assessment procedures—implementation of continuous comprehensive procedures and recording students' progress i.e., cumulative record; Developing model test items which are competency specific model test papers; Quality issues under Right to Education (RTE) and implementation of Continuous and Comprehensive Evaluation (CCE) in schools.

In these classes the teachers were taught to offer their learners collaborative opportunities in planning and reading processes. The teachers were also taught the ability of improving retention and recollection in connection with textual activities. The participants were trained in aspects related to pair work, group work and complementary relationship; acquiring skills and developing one's own skills; learning from others and identifying learning opportunities; learning from others and participating in the creative process of seeking support and feedback; drills for perfection; overcoming shyness, mentoring and supervising; knowing oneself; being oneself with others; art of acknowledgement of planning and execution; getting comfortable; understanding learning styles, etc.

Some of the classes exemplified leaner-centered learning and demonstrated to the participants through the use of games and activities what can be incorporated in the class. Some classes focused on theory and practice relationship and the requirement to fine-tune research based techniques to language teaching making allowance for ground realities. On the other hand, the classes also focused on the requirement to break with tradition and overcome local hindrances to incorporate strategies proposed by APSWREIS through TD Programmes. In conclusion, in-service teachers felt motivated and were advised to incorporate the strategies that they imbibed from T D programmes upon return to their respective schools run by APSWREIS.

Therefore, it has been noted by the researcher that the TD Programmes were organised at various institutes which are of high reputation. The participants who belonged to the APSWREIS were put up at the institutes. The sessions at the TDPs were dealt with by resource persons of various fields of the English language. There were various discussions pertaining to the problems that were faced by the student - teacher community at the APSWREIS. Many a participant at the TDPs talked about student-centered learning and the problems that they had encountered, mainly in large classes. Furthermore, many a Resource person was observed addressing actual classroom situation faced by the teacher. There were regular sessions for the participants conducted by the Resource persons to explore and analyze organisational factors and amendments undertaken by the state government. The sessions at the TDPs had debating approaches, activities and practical sessions. The participants were informed that they should learn how to incorporate LSRW (listening, speaking, reading, and writing) abilities into a particular hour, within the framework of a textbook centered lesson. The sessions at the TDPs have been observed opposing teaching individual abilities in separate classes, and suggesting to import methods that would assist in figuring out how to combine the different abilities.

Subsequently, to this, some of the teachers opined that the Resource persons need to design the learning approaches collectively in common to depict how an individual lesson can integrate all of the four language abilities at the same time and regularly as opposed to a fragmented strategy. There were responses like, the TDPs should organise sessions on how to assimilate all of the communicative methods effectually. Moreover, some of the APSWREIS teachers complained that they cannot take ample freedom in their real time classroom environment due to the organisational structure, its rules and regulations. The teachers, further, have responded that they would firmly communicate to the administration about the constraints that they are facing while teaching in the APSWREIS schools.

A participant is found mentioning that most of the sessions at the TDPs and the outline of the programmes there are especially good, but then again these methods cannot be incorporated due to the functionalism of the school system. It has been observed that several teachers expressed their concern that they might be under pressure to discontinue their initiatives to modify methodologies in their actual classroom situation. It has been commented by several participants that they were pondering about the way in which they could implement the strategies learnt at the TDP sessions when they go back to their classrooms.

Consequently, it has been observed by the researcher that there was hardly any discussion of second language acquisition research and theory in the TDPs. The researcher was only able to see a casual introduction to second language acquisition theory in one of the sessions. As a matter of fact, in one of the semi-structured interviews with a Resource person, it was opined that there was a definite need to avoid laying emphasis on theory as it seemed disconnected from the classroom when related to objectives on particular and relevant methodologies. A Resource person mentioned the significance of a mentoring structure. When the teachers leave the TDP training institutes, they may have handled one or two sample lessons in front of a group of teachers, not in real classroom situation. However, in the observation of the researcher, the APSWREIS administration could not follow-up regarding the training abilities and the methodologies gained by the teacher at the TDPs. The Resource persons are found suggesting the participants should keep follow-up for themselves while they are experimenting with the learned theories in their classrooms. Some teachers informed that after they go back to their schools, they are pressurised between completing the syllabus and rushing effectively for local needs in an exam-driven culture.

One Resource person is found suggesting that the teachers have to think from the learners' point of view. The participants are to play a role as learners in the in-service teacher enrichment programme. The programme was observed addressing teaching methods and teaching materials etc. Even though we have equivalent words in the mother tongue, we as teachers are not using them in the classrooms; the speech stressed the usage of mother tongue in English language classrooms.

The APSWREIS teachers at the TDPs were taken gradually through the process of reflective teaching. The teachers were taught to have listening and speaking skills designed and instructed through particular models (difference between listening in real life and listening in the English classroom, sub-skills of listening, practice, stages in a listening lesson, principles of CLT, methods and materials of speaking) and to correlate with their teaching material to make certain whether they succeeded in their objectives or not. One another programme at the Andhra Pradesh Academy of Rural Development (APARD) had classes entitled "Teacher Development Programme Modules: Reading Wise Programme." The classes dealt with reading instruction methods. In these classes, the participants were introduced to several kinds of reading and some of the factors were in tune with teaching methods. The teachers were briefed about the philosophy of new text books, viz., the basic principles based on which the text books were developed; Subject specific academic standards/competencies or attainment targets were recommended in the text books and for the teaching learning process; Planning – Annual and unit cum lesson plans; Demonstration of Model lessons focusing on the steps for teaching; People assessment procedures—implementation of continuous comprehensive procedures and recording students' progress i.e., cumulative record; Developing model test items which are competency specific model test papers; Quality issues under Right to Education (RTE) and implementation of Continuous and Comprehensive Evaluation (CCE) in schools.

The participants were motivated to continually educate themselves on their knowledge of grammatical rules but warned nevertheless not to teach grammar in inflexible step-by-step modes, isolated from actual usage. Some of the classes exemplified leaner-centered learning and demonstrated to the participants through the use of games and activities that can be incorporated in the class. Some classes focused on theory and practice relationship and the requirement to fine-tune research based techniques to language teaching making allowance for realities on the ground. On the other hand, the classes also focused on the requirement to break traditions and overcome local hindrances to incorporate strategies proposed by the APSWREIS through T D Programmes.

Therefore, in-service teachers felt motivated and advised to incorporate the strategies that they imbibed from TD programmes upon return to their respective schools run by APSWREIS. A particular circular issued by the authorities concentrates on the issue of maintaining teaching diaries. The teachers were asked to include the details of "conduct of tests, examination assignment, practical, remedial classes, extra classes, study hours, counselling etc." Furthermore, the document mentions that the teachers are ordered to remodel the maintenance of teaching notes, tell about teaching methodology, structure of the topic and its division in terms of the question paper pattern. However, the coverage of topics need not be mentioned in the teaching notes daily. Most of the documents were intended for developing English speaking and writing skills of teachers working in APSWREIS. Furthermore, the documents are issued as circulars for teachers dealing with V, VI, & VII Class – to develop their teaching skills in multiple intelligences. One document is a circular issued to the teachers to attend an orientation-training programme on new textbooks assessment procedures (CCE) lesson plans and steps for teaching. APSWREIS has organised T D programmes for in-service English teachers that run for 4 - 14 days. One of the agendas of this study was on the 04 - 14 day programmes, which were documented during 2007 – 2014. By and large, the 04 – 14 day programmes are attended by a group of teachers (between 10 - 40) from various schools run by APSWREIS. The participants are housed in AMR – APARD, EFLU and other campuses situated in Hyderabad for the prescribed time. Teachers working at various schools run by APSWREIS located in various districts are sent invitations (Memos and Circulars) to attend T D Programmes. Generally, participants from various districts are represented at a time and are put together as a group. During the investigator's time at the campuses, it was possible to observe the groups comprising of 10 - 40 teachers.

These campuses provide accommodation. The campuses are equipped with language labs, computer labs, lecture halls, and classrooms. The computers in the language labs are comparatively modern as compared to the computers in the computer labs. The classrooms in which the TD programmes were organised were all equipped with projectors that connect to the resource persons' laptops for multimedia presentations. There are correspondingly extremely well stocked libraries with books on many subtopics in the field of English language education in all the campuses. There are literary resources, and books on grammar, phonetics, writing, reading, educational theory, psychology, and teacher training. The library collections are indeed impressive. As mentioned, classes for the participants begin at 9:30 a.m. The classes regularly start with an introduction on teaching methods and teaching materials. Following this, there are presentations on listening, speaking, reading and writing skills. The in-service teachers are expected to participate in Drill and Mock teaching Sessions. They are given assignments. Each session lasts two hours. During the course of the day, the in-service teachers are to pay attention to the lectures. Moreover, they are expected to prepare lesson plans, participate in Reading Wise Programmes, role play and discussion. The sessions had activities, viz., integrated skill activities, oral fluency activities, hearing and watching stories/songs/videos. These activities were to be performed in the lecture mode – where the teachers had to handle the activities independently through prescribed topics. The topics focused primarily on listening and speaking. The teachers had to carry out assignments that assess them on their acquaintance with the phonetics and the nuances of phonetics. Following this, in-service teachers were introduced to strategies of teaching English to the second language learner, viz., handouts on teaching vocabulary, where the teacher is intended to search for resources and write one of their assignments; Ticking of items; detecting mistakes; guessing definitions; topic based and task based activity; pronunciation games and so on.

All the participants are made to form groups and perform activities, viz.; Grammar based activity, where in-service teachers work on grammar exercises from handouts provided; Group Work; Problem Solving and Decision Making. The sessions for in-service teachers mainly focus on the issue of Teacher Development. In one of the sessions, participants were made to focus on teaching learning strategies. Moreover, these techniques in a sense appear recommended by the resource persons for employing in teachers' classrooms. Correspondingly, many a session at the campuses focused on learner factors, viz., student-centered learning; developing relationships; being learner friendly; enhancing interest and enthusiasm in students; strengthening student speech and output, and the importance of the techniques for learning. The sessions also focused on the requirement for constant teacher development and resources that in-service teachers can utilise once the T D programme is completed. The in-service teachers were shown how to design lessons plans, criteria for evaluating a speaking lesson and make changes to their teaching. Further, the sessions introduced in-service teachers to some of the fundamentals of vocabulary in Second Language Acquisition. The participants were also presented with cognitive, meta-cognitive, and socio-cultural theories of English language learning.

One of the programmes at EFLU campus had sessions entitled "Teacher Enrichment Programme Modules: Theory and Reflection." These sessions focused mainly on reflective teaching and action research. The in-service teachers were taken gradually through the process of reflective teaching. The participants were counseled to have listening and speaking abilities designed and instructed through particular models (difference between listening in real life and listening in the English classroom, sub-skills of listening, practice, stages in a listening lesson, principles of CLT, methods and materials of speaking) and to correlate with their teaching material to make certain whether they succeeded in their objectives or not. The participants were also advised to reflect upon the approaches/guidelines for the design of listening tasks and speaking. In reference to action research, the in-service teachers were asked to explicate the challenges of conducting a speaking activity and design a plan of action as to how to address specific classroom issues.

Another programme at EFLU campus had sessions entitled "Teacher Development Programme Modules: Communication Skills." In this programme in-service teachers were asked to enhance the speaking and reading abilities of students in a more interactive mode. The participants were taught how to make students use visual images. The participants were further asked to do pre-reading activities. These activities were regarded as supporting the teachers' in real time classroom teaching students about comprehension. The sessions discussed the significance of experiential and constructivist methods in the teaching of reading and speaking, where teachers were expected to tap into the background knowledge of learners and offer student-centered tasks to promote communication skills. Most of the sessions focused on the significance of a range of instructional methods employed to move learners gradually towards a better understanding and, in the long run, more objectivity in the learning procedures. The teachers were instructed on how a teacher should lead students through challenging readings to reduce nervousness that regularly goes along with English language teaching.

The programme at the Andhra Pradesh Academy of Rural Development (APARD) had sessions entitled "Teacher Development Programme Modules: Reading Wise Programme." The sessions were focused on reading instruction. In these sessions, in-service teachers were introduced to the various kinds of reading and some of the aspects were in tune with teaching methods. The participants were briefed about the philosophy of new text books i.e., the basic principles based on which the text books were developed; Subject specific academic standards/ competencies or attainment targets were recommended in the text books and for the teaching learning process; Planning – Annual and unit cum lesson plans; Demonstration of Model lessons focusing on the steps for teaching; People assessment procedures—implementation of continuous comprehensive procedures and recording students' progress i.e., cumulative record; Developing model test items which are competency specific model test papers; Quality issues under Right to Education (RTE) and implementation of Continuous and Comprehensive Evaluation (CCE) in schools.

In these sessions the teachers were counselled to offer their learners collaborative opportunities in planning and reading processes. The teachers were also taught the ability of improving retention and recollection in connection with textual activities. In-service teachers were trained in aspects, related to pair work, group work and complementary relationship; acquiring skills and developing one is own skills; Learning from others and Identifying Learning Opportunities; learning from others and participating in the creative process of seeking support and feedback; drills for perfection; overcoming shyness, mentoring and supervising; knowing self; being oneself while with others; art of acknowledgement of planning and execution; getting comfortable; understanding learning styles, etc.

The sessions recommended that in-service teachers employ a descriptive method to teach grammar as opposed to a prescriptive method that holds foreign standards above native English language standards. The in-service teachers were motivated to make sure that they employed all the tools accessible to them to create input that was easy for to the learners. Outside of grammar teaching, the discussions on language work, and group work focused on the necessity to make learners speak and read. In some sessions, in-service teachers were encouraged to focus on the requirement to fine-tune text book application to the situation of the classroom and the requirement to bring joint activities into grammar teaching. Some of the sessions exemplified leaner-centered learning and demonstrated to the participants through the use of games and activities that can be incorporated in the class. Some sessions focused on theory and practice relationship and the requirement to fine-tune research based techniques to language teaching making allowance for realities on the ground. On the other hand, the sessions also focused on the requirement to break traditions and overcome local hindrances to incorporate strategies proposed by the APSWREIS through T D Programmes. In conclusion, in-service teachers felt motivated and advised to incorporate the strategies that they imbibed from TD programmes upon return to their respective schools run by APSWREIS.

Chapter - 5

Class Room Practices

Classroom observation was undertaken as part of the research. The classes were video recorded and later analysed using two observation schedules. This chapter presents the findings of the different analyses done for ten teachers. The first part presents a quantitative assessment using the classroom observation schedule prepared by Gray and Lambert (1976). In the second part, a qualitative analysis is presented. Within this, a broad description is given of three lessons/classes each of 10 teachers. Following this, an in-depth analysis of four teachers' classroom practices is presented. The observation schedule prepared by Gray and Lambert (1976). This instrument assists in noting whether an aspect is present or absent (yes or no). It consists of sections on teachers' language proficiency, their preparation, the content of the material used in the classroom by them, teaching methods and approaches adopted by them, pedagogical content, classroom management, teacher qualities, their delivery and presentation, rapport and interaction with students, sensitivity towards learners, summarisation, evaluation of learning, relating one lesson with other lessons and fulfilling the objectives teaching the text. The general purpose of the observations was to allow the researcher to understand and comment on issues related to the following questions. There are sixteen sections to the observation schedule.

Section 1: Language Proficiency

Item 1.1: This item of the Observation Schedule intended to find out the proficiency of practicing English Teachers' in English language while teaching in classroom.

Language proficiency

The teacher is proficient in English

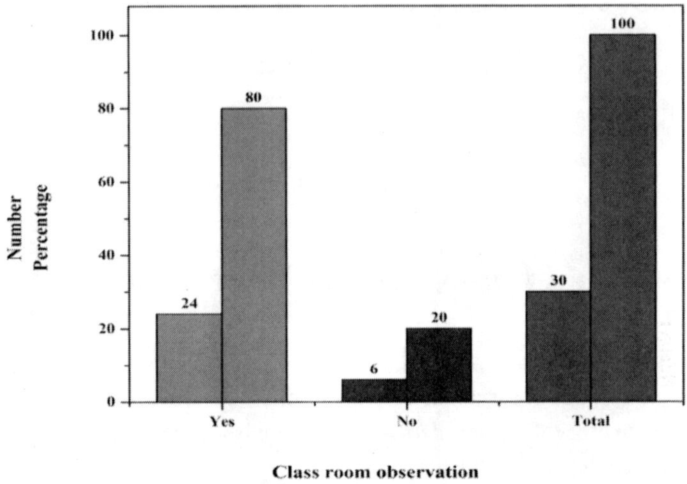

Classroom Observation

Number		%
Yes	24	80
No	6	20
Total	30	100

In the observation schedule the first item pertained to the language proficiency of practicing English teachers. Three regular classes of each English teacher were observed and out of 10 teachers, eight were proficient in the English language while teaching the class. The remaining two did not have adequate proficiency.

To conclude, it may be mentioned that the above section on language proficiency has one observation on the topic related to teacher's proficiency in the English language. Among those English Teachers who responded 80% were observed to be proficient, while 20% were not proficient in language.

Section 2: Preparation

There were two items under this category.

Item 2.1: This item of the Observation Schedule was intended to check if the objectives and purposes of the lesson were clearly expressed by the teacher while teaching.

Preparation: Item 1

Objectives/purposes of the lesson clearly expressed.

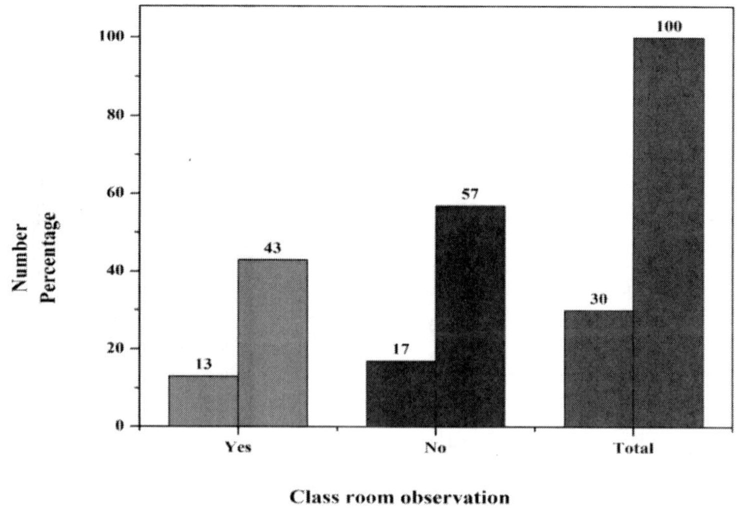

Classroom Observation

Number		
Yes	13	43
No	17	57
Total	**30**	**100**

This item was about stating the objectives of the lesson. Three regular classes of each English teacher were observed. While 43% of teachers expressed the objectives of the lesson, 57% teachers did not mention the objectives of the lesson at the beginning of the lesson.

Item 2.2: This item of the Observation Schedule intended to check if the English Teacher was able to link previous learning of students through relevant examples, analogies etc.

Preparation: Item 2

Linkage to previous experiences and learning established giving relevant examples, analogies etc.

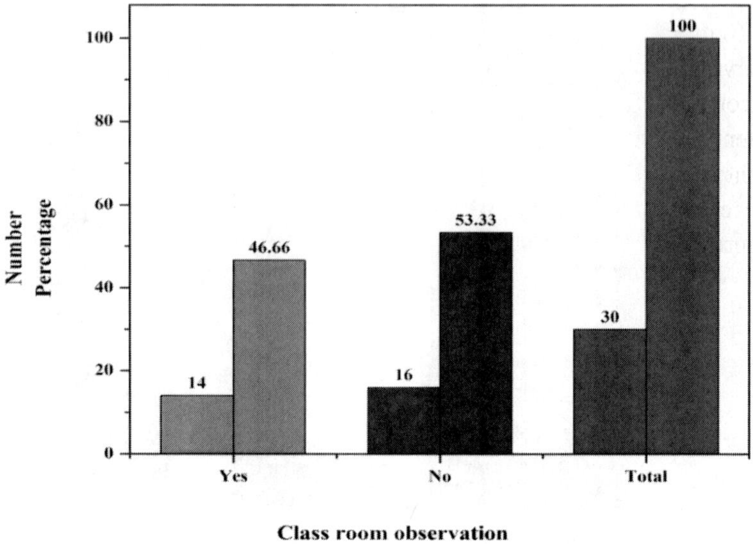

Classroom Observation

Number		%
Yes	14	46.66
No	16	53.33
Total	30	100

This item was about linkage to previous experiences and learning giving relevant examples and analogies. Three regular classes of each teacher were observed and teachers in 14 classes (46.66%) were able to establish a link with previous experiences and learning, through relevant examples and analogies. In the remaining 16 classes (53.33%), teachers did not establish any link between previous lessons and the present ones. Therefore, it may be mentioned that the above section on preparation makes two observations on the topics related to objectives of the lesson clearly expressed and linkage to previous experiences and learning established giving relevant examples. Among the observed Practicing English Teachers, 45% were observed fulfilling the observations mentioned above, while 55% were not fulfilling.

Section 3: Content

There were three items in this section.

Item 3.1: This item of the Observation Schedule was intended to observe English Teachers' teaching methods and their appropriateness to the comprehension level of the students. This item was about teaching content according to the level of student. In 24 classes (80%) teachers taught using language that was appropriate to the level of the students. The remaining 6 classes (20%) were found to be inappropriate to the comprehension level of students.

Content: Item 1

Appropriate to the level of the students

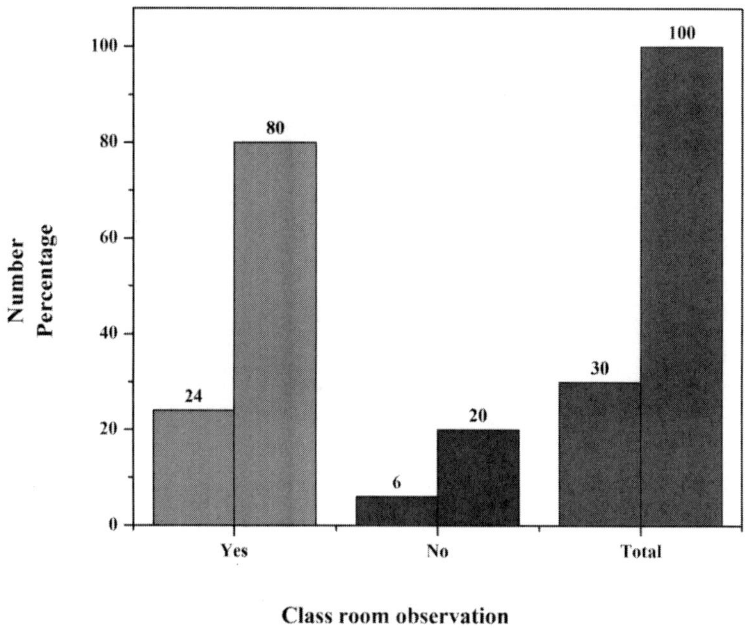

Classroom Observation

Number		%
Yes	24	80
No	6	20
Total	**30**	**100**

Item 3.2: This item of the Observation Schedule was intended to observe relevance of the units to the needs of the students.

Content: Item 2

Relevant to the needs of the students.

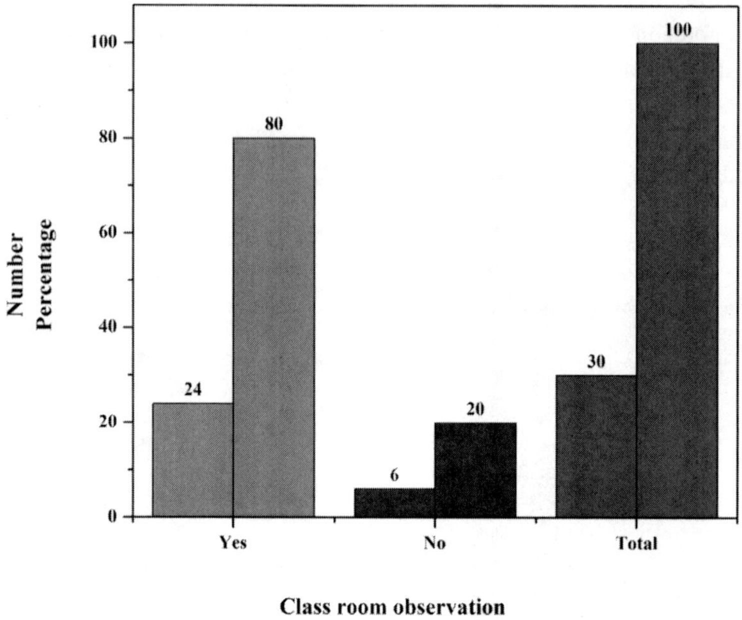

Classroom Observation

Number		%
Yes	24	80
No	6	20
Total	**30**	**100**

This item was about teaching that was relevant to the needs of students. 24 classes (80%) were found to be relevant to the needs of students. The remaining 6 classes (20%) were not found to be relevant to the needs of students.

Item 3.3: This item of the Observation Schedule was intended to observe English Teachers' knowledge of subject matter while teaching.

Content: Item 3

Possessed in-depth knowledge of subject matter.

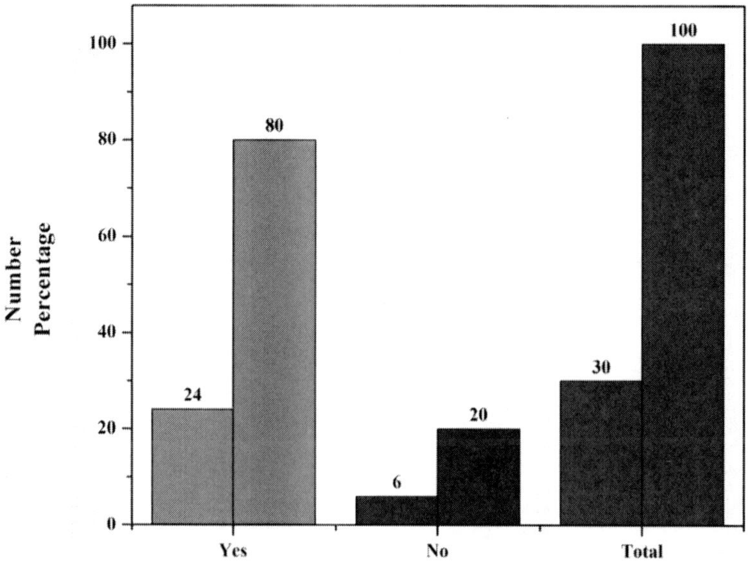

Class room observation

Classroom Observation

Number		%
Yes	24	80
No	6	20
Total	**30**	**100**

This item was about whether teachers possess in-depth knowledge of the subject matter. 24 classes (80%) were taught by the teachers who possessed in-depth knowledge of subject matter. The remaining 6 classes (20%) were not taught by the teachers who had in-depth knowledge of subject. Therefore, it may be mentioned that the above section on content reported three observations on the topics related to appropriateness of the content, relevance to the needs of students and knowledge of subject matter of teachers teaching on the course. Among the observed English Teachers, 80% appeared to fulfill the observations mentioned above, while 20% did not fulfill the same.

Section 4: Teaching Method(s)/Approach(es)

There were two items in this section.

Item 4.1: This item of the Observation Schedule was intended to observe English Teachers' interest in student learning and their adoption of varied methods/approaches and appropriateness of the methods to the situation and learner background.

Teaching method(s)/Approach(es): Item1

Interested in student learning – adapted varied methods/approaches appropriate to the situation and learner background.

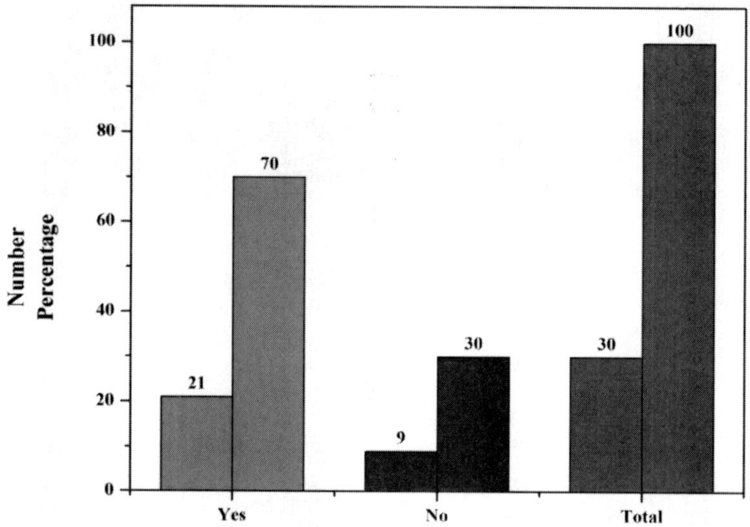

Class room observation

Classroom Observation

Number		%
Yes	21	70
No	9	30
Total	**30**	**100**

This item was about whether the teacher was interested in student learning; adapted varied methods/ approaches appropriate to the teaching context and learner background. 21 classes (70%) were taught by the teachers who were interested in student learning and who adopted varied methods/ approaches appropriate to the context and background of learners. The remaining 6 classes (20%) were taught by teachers who did not adopt varied methods/ approaches appropriate to the situation and learner background.

Item 4.2: This item of the Observation Schedule was intended to observe how well thought out the teaching sessions were. This item was about whether each class was well planned session. 18 classes (60%) were well thought sessions. The remaining 12 classes (40%) were found to be inadequate in terms of planning. Therefore, it may be mentioned that the above section on Teaching Method(s)/Approach (es) focused on how imaginative and interesting teachers made the sessions by adopting varied methods/approaches appropriate to the situation and learner background observed. Of the English Teachers, 70% seemed to fulfill the mentioned above, while 30% did not fulfill it.

Teaching method(s)/Approach(es): Item 2

Well thought out session

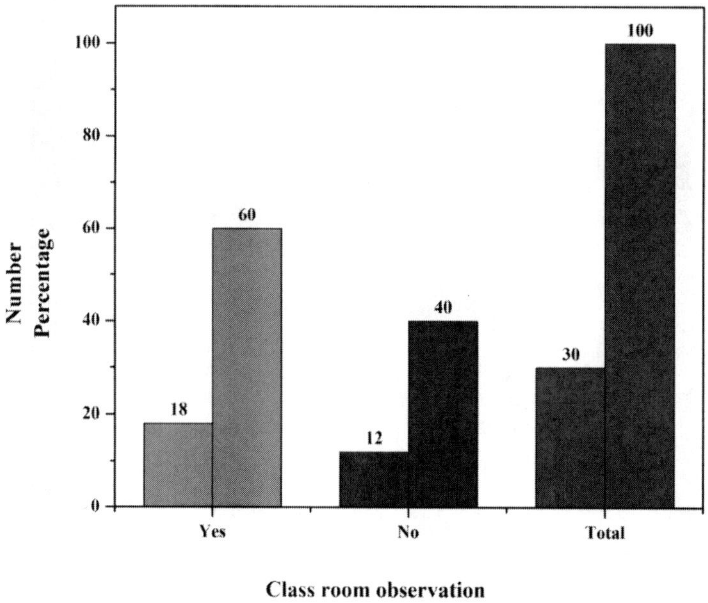

Classroom Observation

Number		%
Yes	18	60
No	12	40
Total	**30**	**100**

Section 5: Teaching-Learning Materials

There were three items in this section.

Item 5.1: This item of the Observation Schedule was intended to observe English Teachers' use of neat and colourful materials while teaching.

Teaching-Learning Materials: Item 1

Neat and colourful.

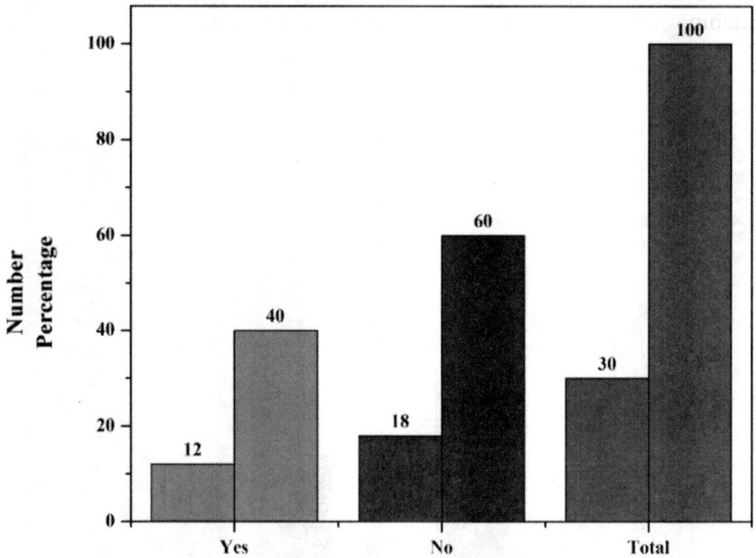

Class room observation

Classroom Observation

Number		%
Yes	12	40
No	18	60
Total	**30**	**100**

This item was about whether teaching-learning materials were neat and colourful. 12 classes (40%) saw students being given neat and colorful teaching-learning materials. The remaining 18 classes (60%) were not found to be using imaginative teaching materials.

Item 5.2: This item of the Observation Schedule intended to find out the appropriateness of teaching materials while the lesson was being taught. This item was about whether Teaching- Learning Materials were appropriate to the lesson taught. In 18 classes (60%) materials used were appropriate to the lesson taught. In the remaining 12 classes, (40%) teaching- learning materials were not appropriate to the lesson taught.

Teaching-Learning Materials: Item 2

Appropriate to the lesson taught.

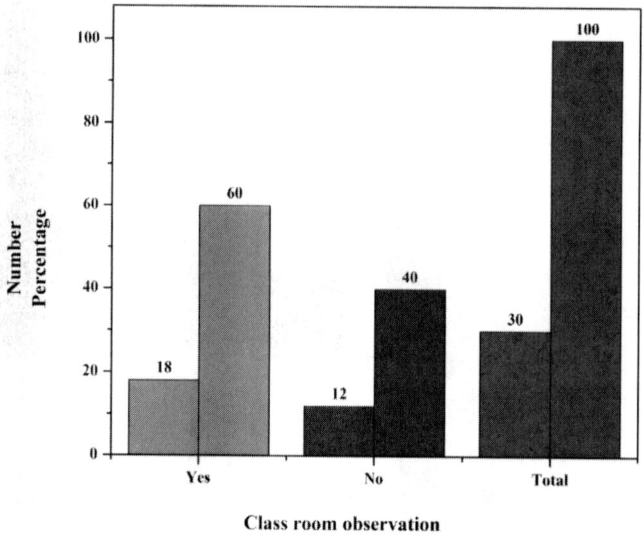

Classroom Observation

Number		%
Yes	18	60
No	12	40
Total	**30**	**100**

Item 5.3: This item of the Observation Schedule was intended to observe for English Teachers' appropriateness in terms of teaching materials. This item was about whether the Teaching- Learning Materials were appropriate to the level of the learners. 18 classes (60%) were appropriate in terms of use of teaching materials that were in keeping with level of learners. The remaining 12 classes (40%) showed that teaching- learning materials used were not appropriate to the level of the learners. Therefore, it may be mentioned that the above section on Teaching-Learning Materials reveals three observations on the topics: maintenance of neatness and colourfulness, materials being appropriate to the levels taught and appealing to learners. Of the English Teachers who were observed, 60% fulfilled the criteria mentioned above, while 40% did not fulfill it.

Teaching-Learning Materials: Item 3
Appropriate to the level of the learners

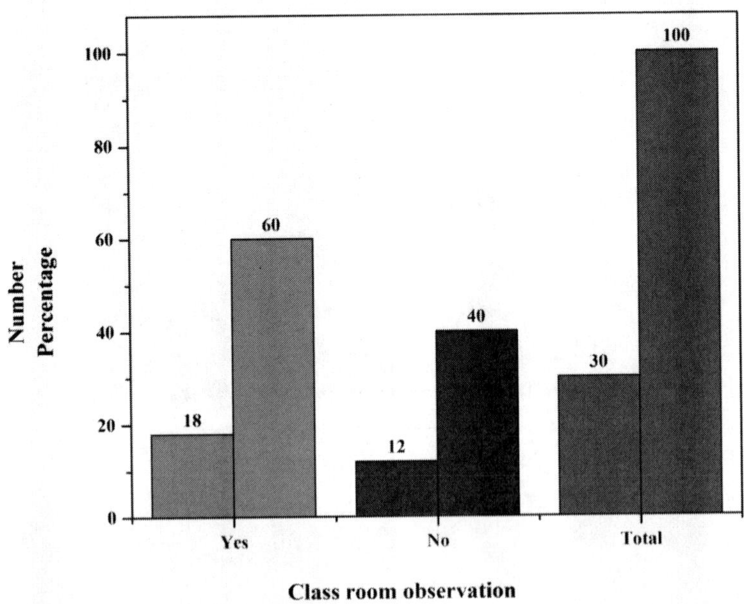

Classroom Observation

Number		%
Yes	18	60
No	12	40
Total	**30**	**100**

Section 6: Pedagogical Content Knowledge

Item 6.1: This item of the Observation Schedule was intended to observe the expression of the nature of language employed by teachers while teaching.

Pedagogical Content Knowledge: Item 1

The nature of the language expressed

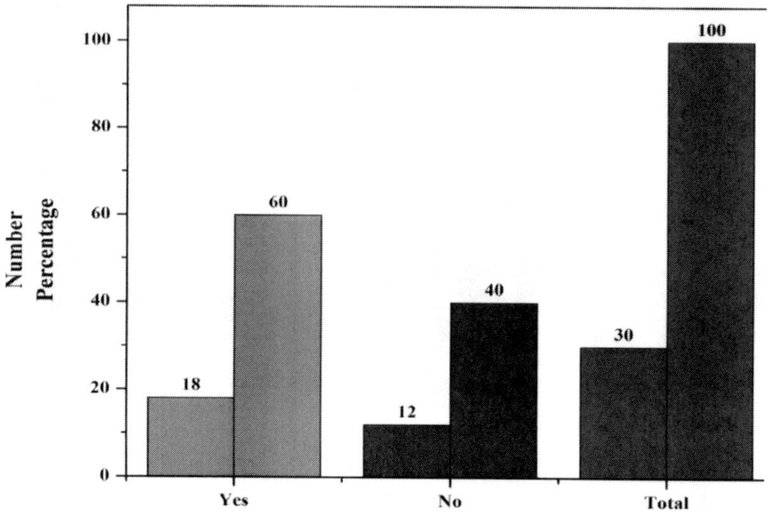

Classroom Observation

Number		%
Yes	18	60
No	12	40
Total	**30**	**100**

This item was about whether the teacher commented on the nature of language. 18 classes (60%) saw teachers use fluent English and the remaining 12 classes (40%) did not show teachers demonstrating fluency in using English.

Item 6.2: This item of the Observation Schedule was intended to observe the English Teachers' knowledge of learners' understanding being taught

Pedagogical Content Knowledge: Item 2

Had knowledge of learners' understandings and misunderstanding of topics

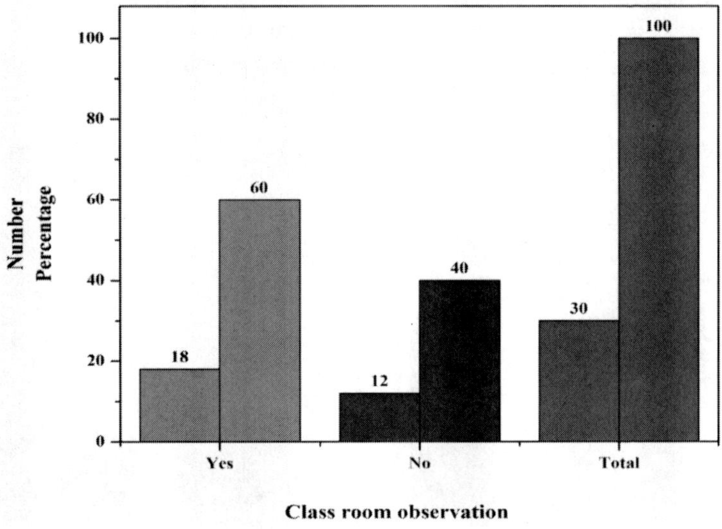

Classroom Observation

Number		%
Yes	18	60
No	12	40
Total	**30**	**100**

This item was about whether the teacher had knowledge of learners' comprehension. 18 classes (60%) were taught by the teachers who had knowledge of learners' background knowledge of topics. The remaining 12 classes (40%) were not taught with any awareness of learners' knowledge of topics.

Item 6.3: This item of the Observation Schedule was intended to observe English teachers' question forms and explanations. This item was about what kind of questions teachers put to learners. 18 classes (60%) saw teachers ask a variety of questions to test students' comprehension of the concept taught in the class. The remaining 12 classes (40%) saw teachers ask only yes-no questions that were of little use to test comprehension. The teachers in these 12 classes seemed to lack command of the subject and the adequate proficiency in English to ask information questions that could elicit different kinds of open-ended answers.

Pedagogical Content Knowledge: Item 3

Questioning and explanation was logical

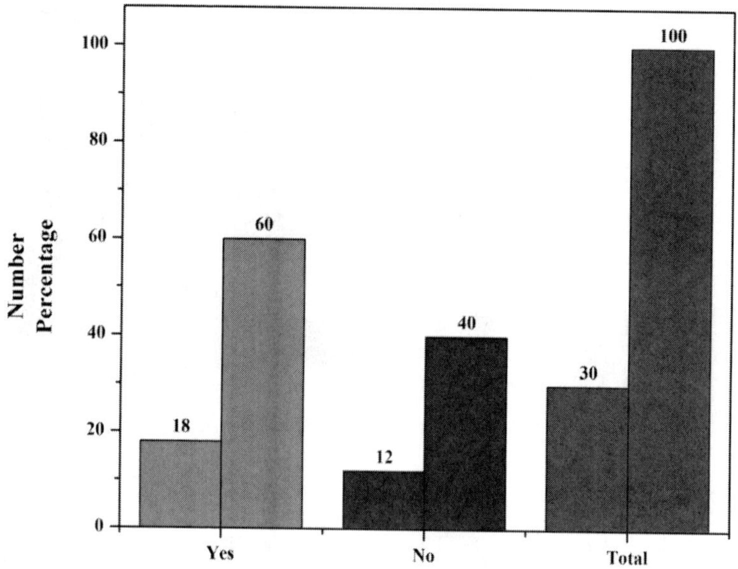

Class room observation

Classroom Observation

Number		%
Yes	18	60
No	12	40
Total	**30**	**100**

Item 6.4: This item of the Observation Schedule was intended to observe if teachers had used students' contributions effectively while teaching.

Pedagogical Content Knowledge: Item 4

Student contributions used effectively

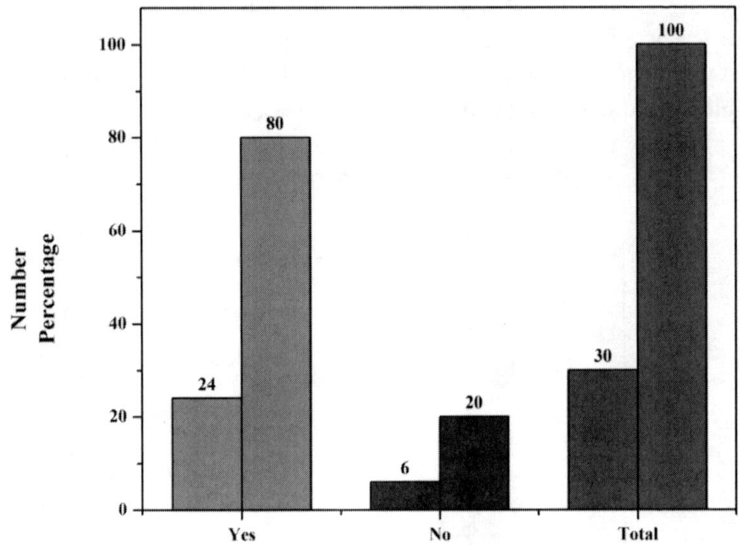

Class room observation

Classroom Observation

Number		%
Yes	24	80
No	6	20
Total	**30**	**100**

This item was about whether the student contributions were used effectively. 24 classes (80%) used student contributions effectively. The remaining 6 classes (20%) did not use student contributions effectively.

Item 6.5: This item of the Observation Schedule was intended to find out if English Teachers' have knowledge of curriculum and curricular materials while teaching.

Pedagogical Content Knowledge: Item 5

Possessed knowledge of curriculum and curricular materials

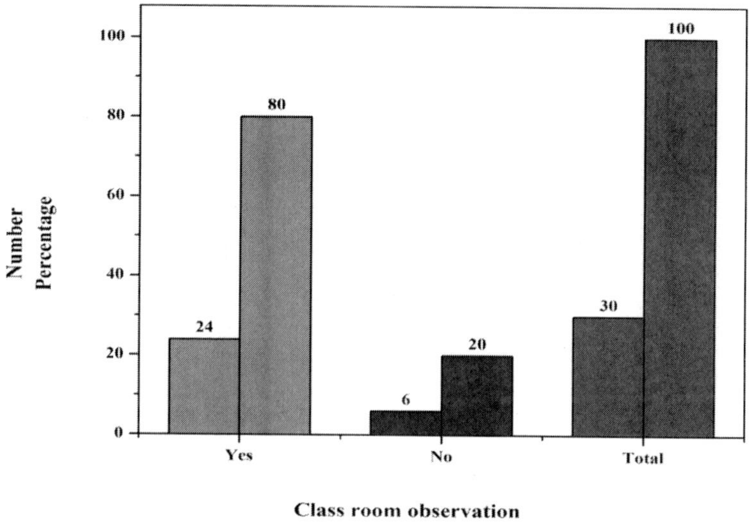

Classroom Observation

Number		%
Yes	24	80
No	6	20
Total	**30**	**100**

This item was about whether the teacher possessed knowledge of curriculum and curricular materials. 24 classes (80%) saw teachers who had knowledge of curriculum and curricular materials. The remaining 6 classes (20%) had teachers who did not possess knowledge of curriculum and curricular materials.

Item 6.6: This item of the Observation Schedule was intended to observe English Teachers' knowledge of strategies for teaching language. This item was about whether the teacher possessed knowledge of strategies for teaching language. In 18 classes (60%) it was apparent that teachers had knowledge of strategies for teaching language. The remaining 12 classes (40%) saw teachers who did not have knowledge of strategies for teaching language. Therefore, it may be mentioned that the above section on Pedagogical Content Knowledge makes six observations on the topics: expressing the nature of the language, having knowledge of learners' understandings and misunderstandings of topics, the nature of questioning and explanation being logical, students' contributions being used effectively, possessing knowledge of curriculum, curricular materials, strategies for teaching language. It is found that 63% of the Practicing English Teachers fulfill the observations mentioned above, while 37% do not.

Pedagogical Content Knowledge: Item 6

Possessed knowledge of strategies for teaching language

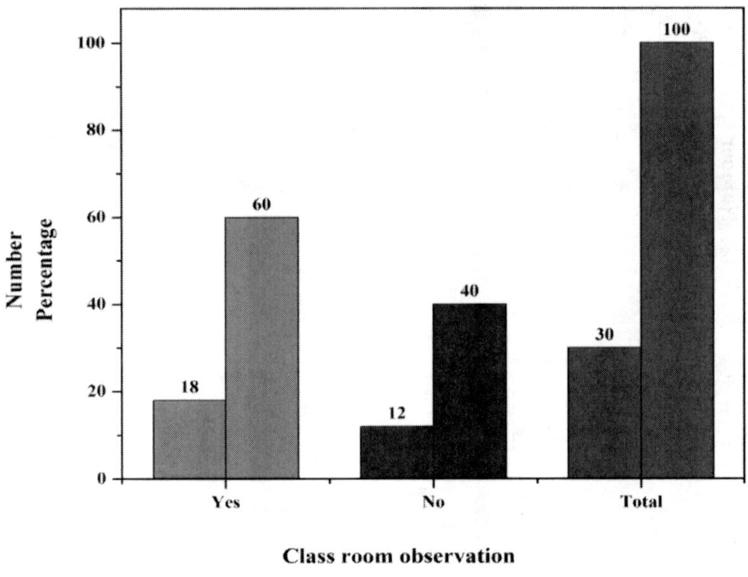

Classroom Observation

Number		%
Yes	18	60
No	12	40
Total	**30**	**100**

Section 7: Classroom Management

Item 7.1: This item of the Observation Schedule was intended to observe English teachers to check if they were able to control students effectively while teaching. This item was about whether the students were controlled effectively. 27 classes (90%) teachers were able to control students effectively. The remaining 3 classes (10%) had teachers who were not able to control the students effectively.

Classroom Management : Item 1

Students were controlled effectively

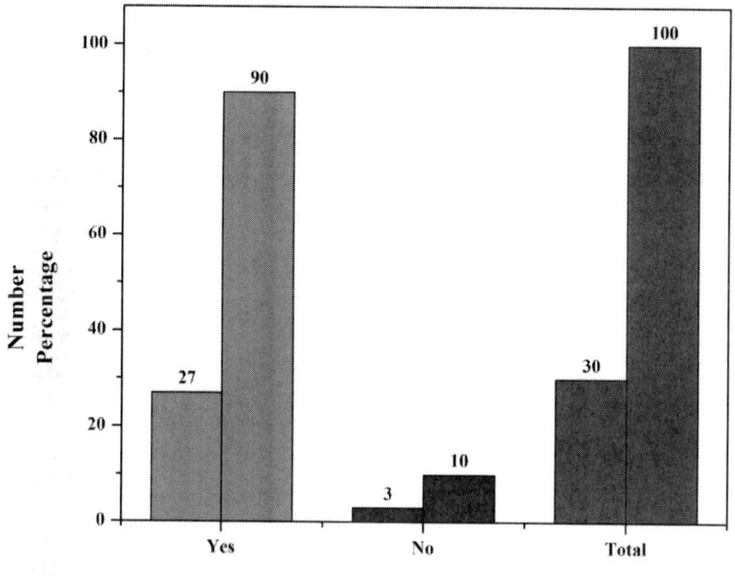

Class room observation

Classroom Observation

Number		%
Yes	27	90
No	3	10
Total	**30**	**100**

Item 7.2: This item of the Observation Schedule was intended to check if English teachers were able to motivate students while teaching. This item was about whether motivation was sustained among students. 19 classes (63.34%) had teachers who were able to motivate students. The remaining 11 classes (36.66%) had teachers who failed to motivate students.

Classroom Management : Item 2

Motivation clearly maintained

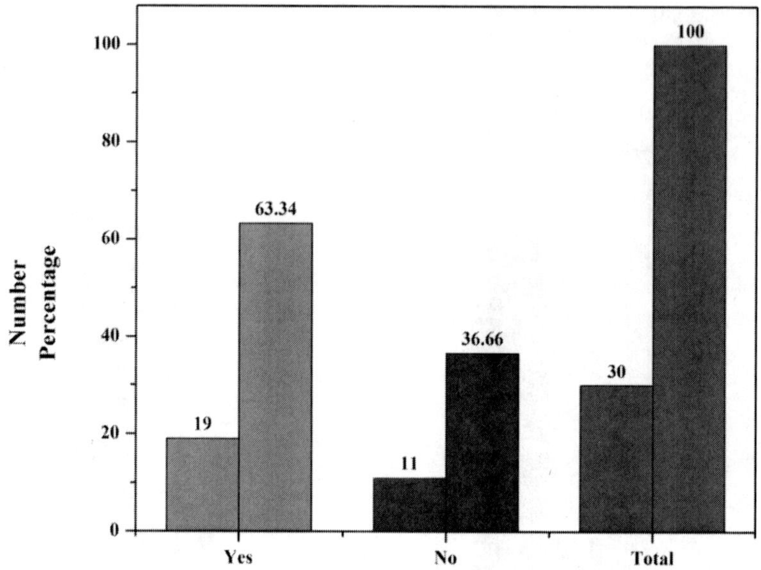

Class room observation

Classroom Observation

Number		%
Yes	19	63.34
No	11	36.66
Total	**30**	**100**

Item 7.3: This item of the Observation Schedule was intended to check whether a particular ambience facilitated learning.

This item was about whether the teachers provided an environment that facilitated learning. 13 classes (43.34%) had a learning environment which facilitated learning. The remaining 17 classes (56.66%) had teachers who were unable to provide an environment that facilitated learning.

Classroom Management : Item 3

Environment facilitated learning.

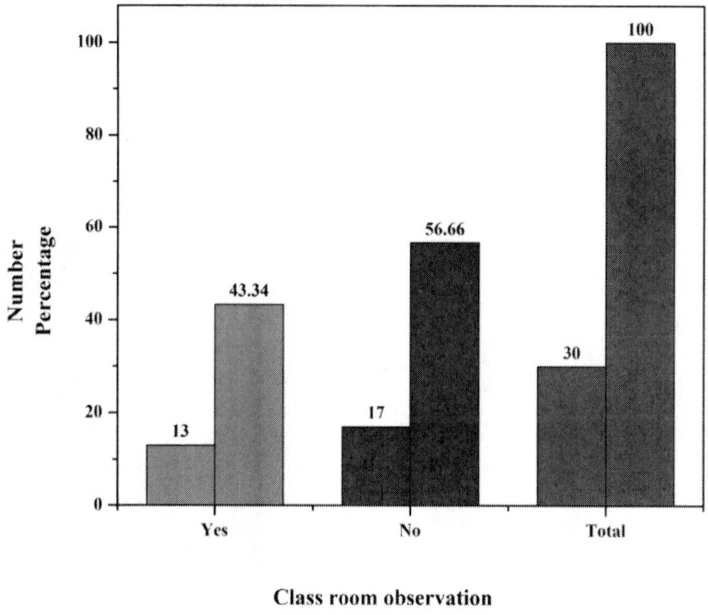

Classroom Observation

Number		%
Yes	13	43.34
No	17	56.66
Total	**30**	**100**

Item 7.4: This item of the Observation Schedule was intended to observe whether the Practicing English Teachers used the class time productively while teaching in the real classroom situation.

This item was about whether class time was used productively. 16 classes (53.34%) saw time class being used productively. The remaining 14 classes (46.66%) saw class time being wasted. Therefore, it may be mentioned that the above section on Classroom Management contains four observations: students being controlled effectively, motivation being sustained, creating environment for learning and classroom time being used productively. The trend among the English teachers showed that 63% fulfilled the observations while 37% did not.

Classroom Management : Item 4

Class time was used productively

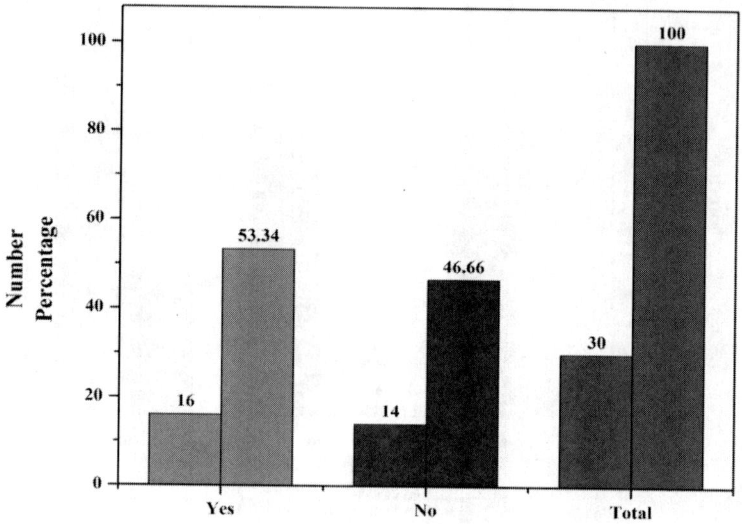

Class room observation

Classroom Observation

Number		%
Yes	16	53.34
No	14	46.66
Total	**30**	**100**

Section 8: Teacher Qualities

This section had three items.

Item 8.1: This item of the Observation Schedule was intended to observe English Teachers' who were enthusiastic about teaching and learning while teaching. This item pertained to whether the teacher was enthusiastic about teaching and learning. 21 classes (70%) had teachers enthusiastic about teaching and learning. The remaining 9 classes

(30%) failed to have the teachers who were enthusiastic for teaching and learning.

Teacher Qualities : Item 1

Enthusiastic for teaching and learning

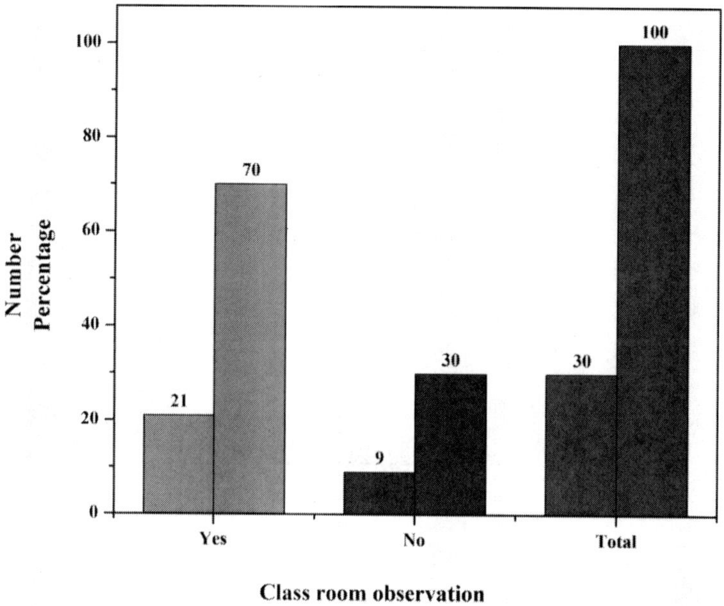

Classroom Observation

Number		%
Yes	21	70
No	9	30
Total	**30**	**100**

Item 8.2: This item of the Observation Schedule was intended to assess the English teachers' confidence while teaching.

This item was about whether the teacher was confident enough to teach. 27classes (90%) were taught by teachers who had confidence. The remaining 3 classes (10%) were not taught by teachers with confidence.

Teacher Qualities : Item 2

Confident

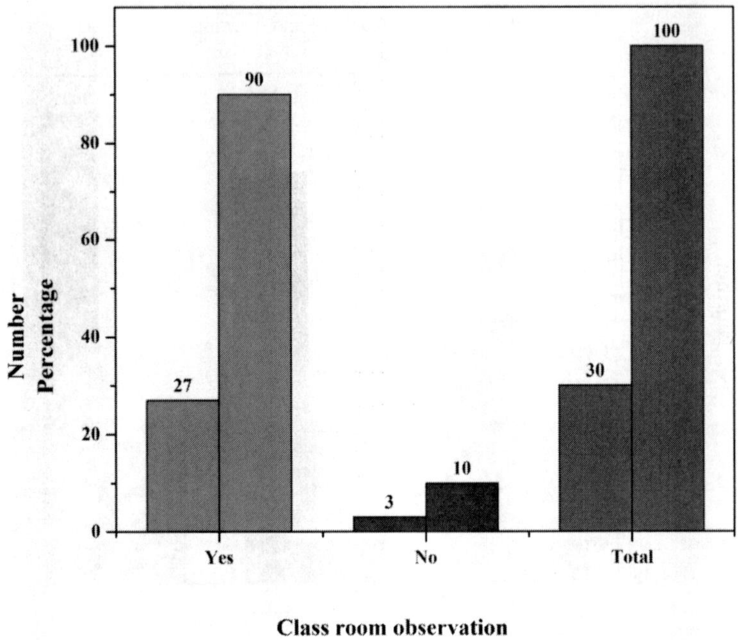

Classroom Observation

Number		%
Yes	27	90
No	3	10
Total	**30**	**100**

Item 8.3: This item of the Observation Schedule was intended to observe English Teachers' who were creative while teaching.

This item was about whether the teacher was Creative. Nine classes had teachers (30%) who were creative. The remaining 21 classes (70%) were not creative in terms of teacher inputs. Therefore, it may be mentioned that the above section on Teacher Qualities considered three parameters: enthusiasm in teachers for teaching and learning, confidence and creativity in teachers when teaching. It may be concluded that 63% of the teachers were found to be creative, while 37% were not.

Teacher Qualities: Item 3

Creative

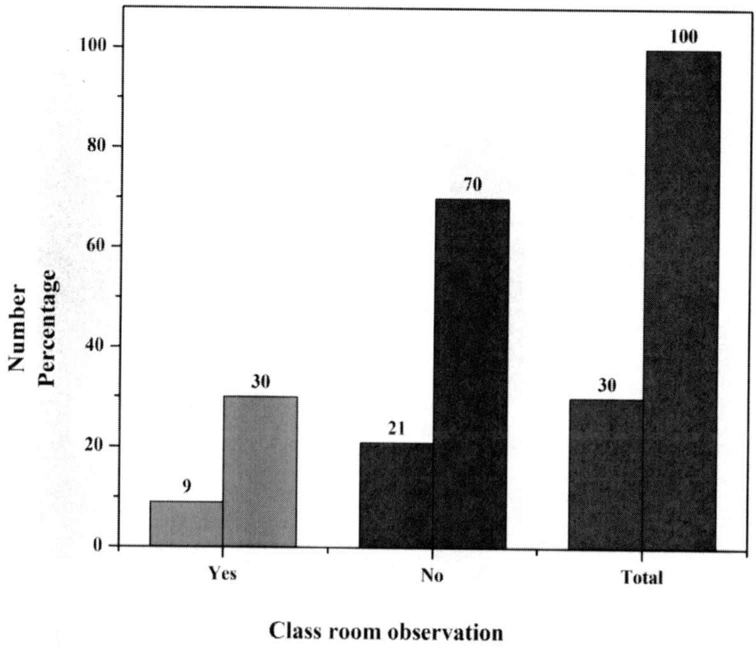

Classroom Observation

Number		%
Yes	9	30
No	21	70
Total	**30**	**100**

Section 9: Delivery and Presentation

Item 9.1: This item of the Observation Schedule was intended to establish if English Teachers organised their teaching and planned it well. This item was about whether the teacher's presentation was well organised. 21 classes (70%) were well-organised. The remaining 9 classes (30%) were not well-organised.

Item 9.2: This item of the Observation Schedule was intended to see if English Teachers' had effective presentation style while teaching.

Delivery and Presentation 2

Presentation style - effective

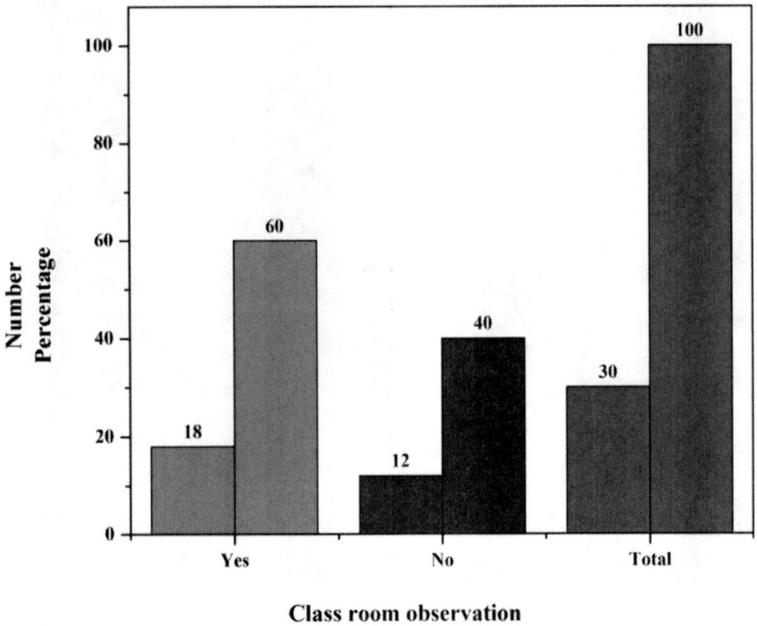

Classroom Observation

Number		%
Yes	18	60
No	12	40
Total	**30**	**100**

This item was about whether the teacher's presentation was effective. 18 classes (60%) showed teachers whose teaching was effective. The remaining 12 classes (40%) were not effective in terms of style.

Item 9.3: This item of the Observation Schedule was intended to see if teachers had clear and audible voice while teaching.

Delivery and Presentation: Item 3

Voice – clear and audible

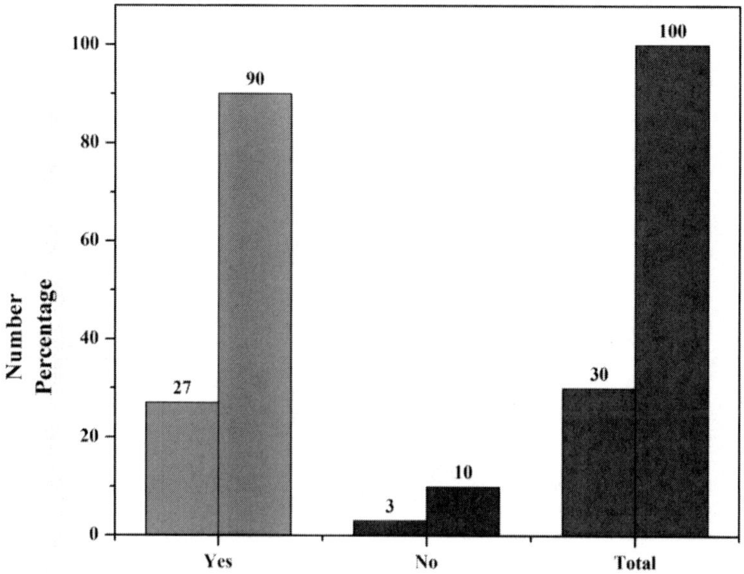

Class room observation

Classroom Observation

Number		%
Yes	27	90
No	3	10
Total	**30**	**100**

This item was about whether the teacher's voice was clear and audible. In 27 classes (90%) the teacher's voice was clear and audible. For the remaining 3 classes (10%) the teacher's voice was not clear or audible.

Item 9.4: This item of the Observation Schedule intended to see if English Teachers used teaching aids that are well produced and effectively used while teaching.

Delivery and Presentation: Item 4

Teaching aids – well produced and used

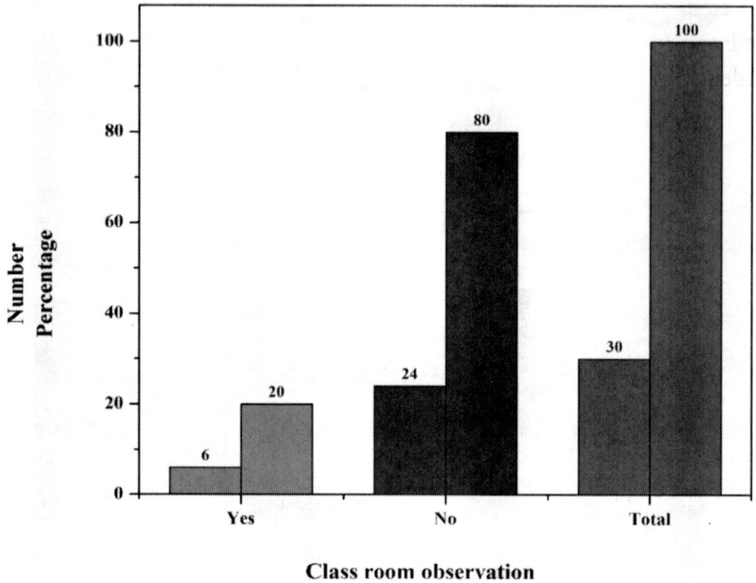

Classroom Observation

Number		%
Yes	6	20
No	24	80
Total	**30**	**100**

This item was about whether the teaching aids were well produced and effectively used. (20%) had teaching aids that were well produced and effectively used. The remaining 24 classes (80%) did not use any teaching aids.

Therefore, it may be mentioned that the above section on Delivery and Presentation contains four parameters: related to (a) well-organised presentation, (b) effective presentation style, (c) clear and audible voice with good production value and (d) effective use of teaching aids in the classroom. The findings show that 60% of the teachers fulfil the criteria while 40% did not.

Section 10: Rapport with Students

There was one item in this section.

Item 10.1: This item of the Observation Schedule intended to study the English Teachers' efforts to maintain warm and friendly relations with students.

Rapport with Students

Warm, accepting, and promoted friendly relations

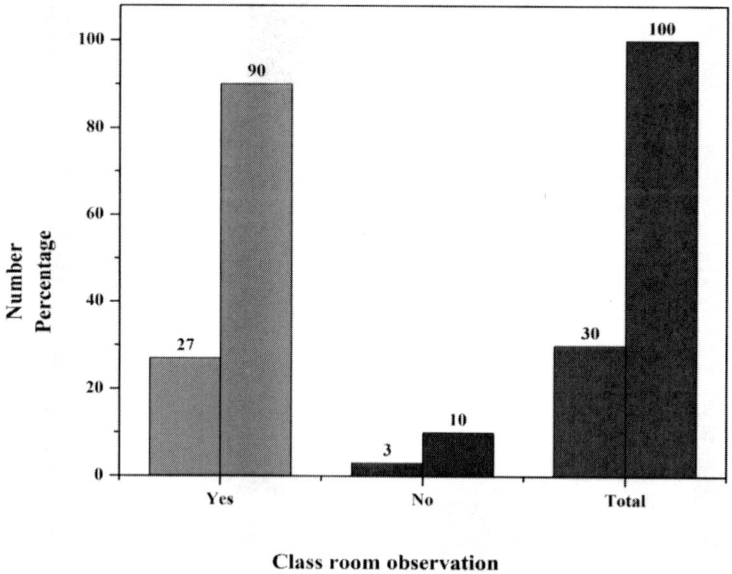

Classroom Observation

Number		%
Yes	27	90
No	3	10
Total	**30**	**100**

This item was whether the teacher was warm, accepting and friendly with students. 27 classes (90%) had warm, accepting and teachers who were friendly relations with students the remaining 3 classes (10%) failed to have warm, accepting and had friendly teachers. Therefore, it may be mentioned that the above section on Rapport with Students was related to the teacher's acceptance and promotion of friendly relations in the classroom. It was observed that 90% of the teachers fulfilled the criteria while only 10% did not.

Section 11: Interaction

Item 11.1: This item of the Observation Schedule intended to assess English Teachers' movement around the classroom with ease and their interaction with students to promote learning while teaching.

Interaction: Item 1

Moved around the classroom with ease, interacted with students and promoted learning

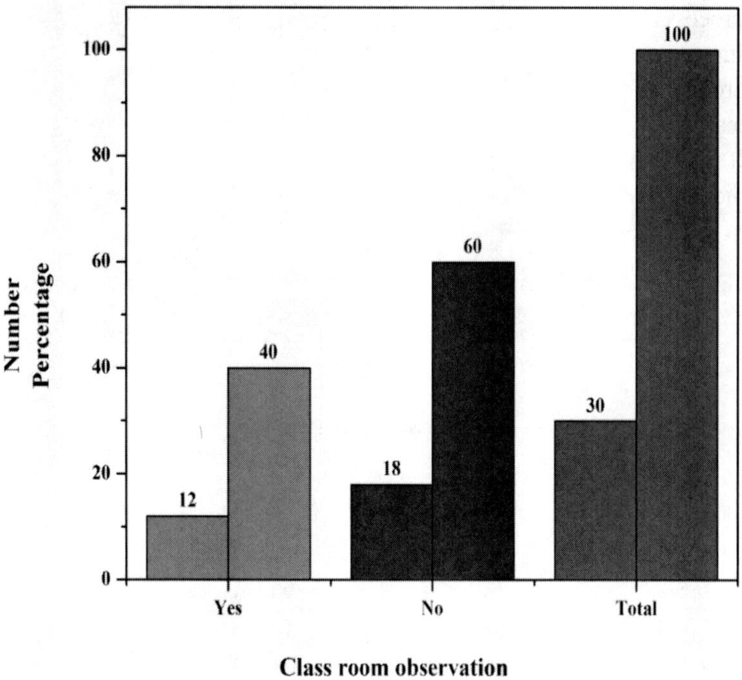

Classroom Observation

	Number	%
Yes	12	40
No	18	60
Total	**30**	**100**

This item was about whether the teacher moved around the classroom with ease, interacted with students and promoted learning. 12 classes (40%) saw the teacher moved around the classroom with ease, interacting with students and promoting learning. The remaining 18 classes (60%) failed to report the teachers moving around interact with students.

Item 11.2: This item of the Observation Schedule was intended to observe the Practicing English Teachers' teaching and students' active involvement in the learning process in the real classroom situation. This item was about whether the teacher has made all the students actively involve themselves in the learning process. 18 classes (60%) had students who were actively involved in the learning process. The remaining 12 classes (40%) saw students who were not actively involved in the learning process. Therefore, it may be mentioned that the above section on Interaction had two parameters on the following aspects: teachers moving around the classroom with ease, interacting with students, promoting learning and students being actively involved in the learning process. It was found that 50% of English Teachers interacted freely while 50% did not.

Interaction: Item 2

All the students actively involved in the learning process

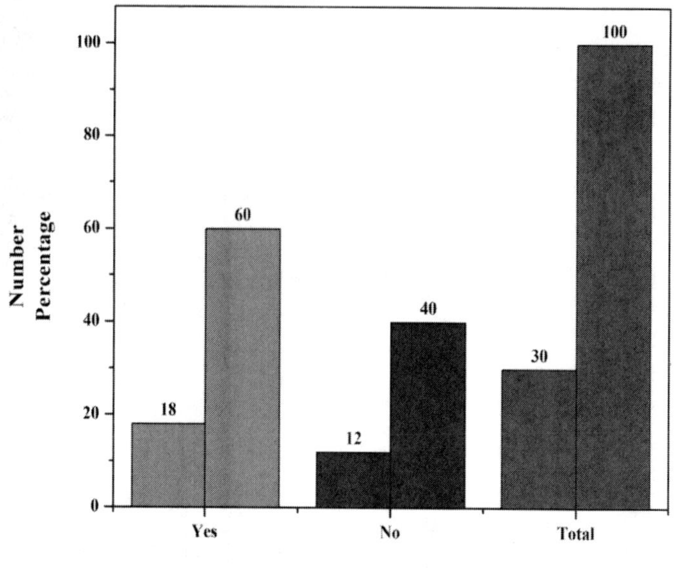

Class room observation

Classroom Observation

Number		%
Yes	18	60
No	12	40
Total	**30**	**100**

Section 12: Sensitivity to Learners

Item 12.1: This item of the Observation Schedule was intended to study Practicing English Teachers' respect for diverse opinions of students.

Sensitivity to Learners: Item 1

Respected diverse opinions

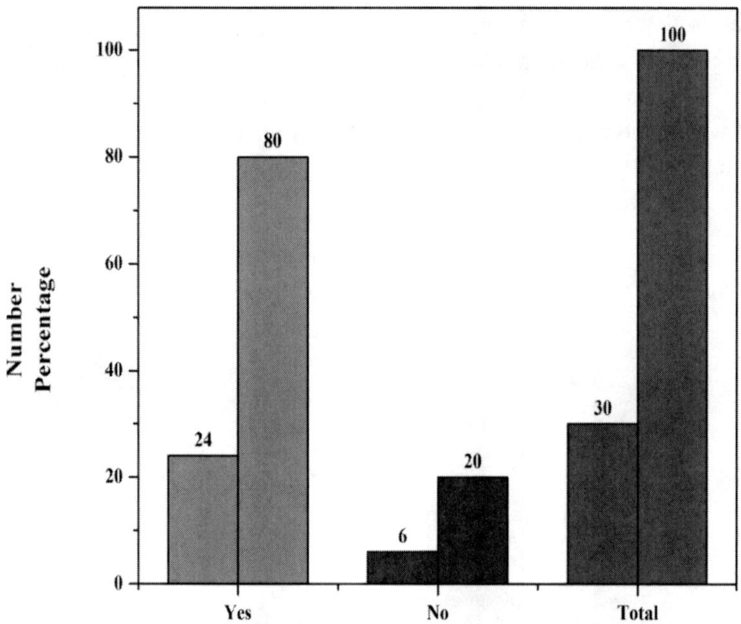

Class room observation

Classroom Observation

Number		%
Yes	24	80
No	6	20
Total	**30**	**100**

This item was about whether the teacher respected diverse opinions from students. 24 classes (80%) had teachers who respected diverse opinions. The remaining 6 classes (20%) teachers who were averse to entertaining opinions.

Item 12.2: This item of the Observation Schedule intended to see if Practicing English Teachers' were sensitive to the feelings of students while teaching.

Sensitivity to Learners: Item 2

Was sensitive to feelings of students

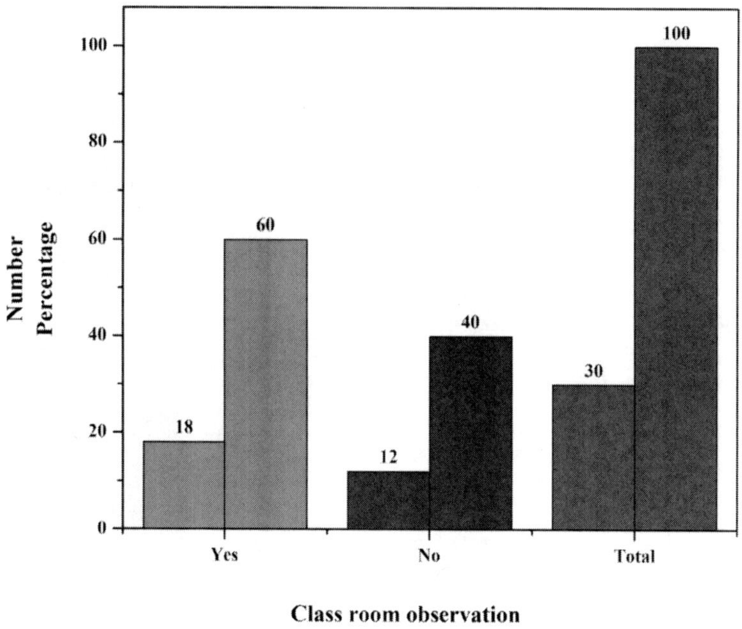

Classroom Observation

Number		%
Yes	18	60
No	12	40
Total	**30**	**100**

This item was about whether the teacher was sensitive to the feelings of students. 18 classes (60%) teachers were sensitive to the feelings of students. The remaining 12 classes (40%) had teachers who were not sensitive to feelings of students.

Item 12.3: This item of the Observation Schedule intended to see if English Teachers' discovered student misunderstanding and misconception about language learning and usage. This item was about whether the teacher discovered student misunderstandings and misconceptions about

Sensitivity to Learners: Item 3

Discovered student misunderstandings and misconceptions of language learning and usage.

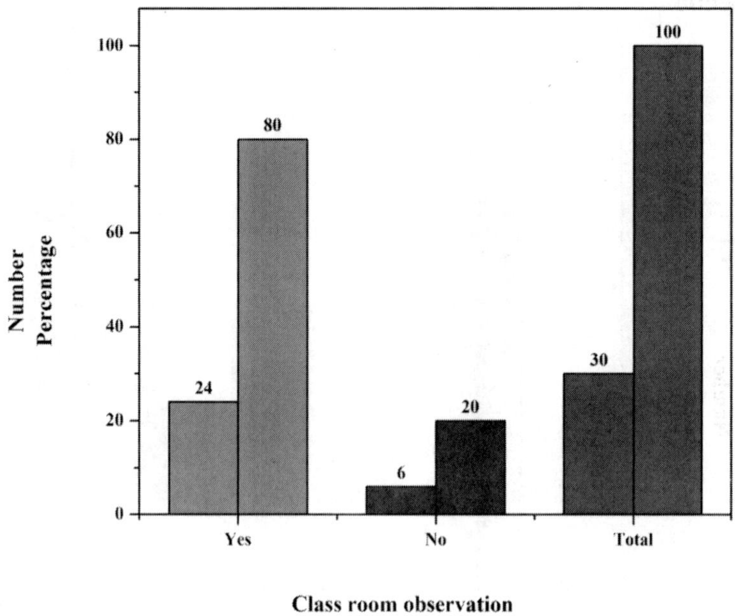

Classroom Observation

Number		%
Yes	24	80
No	6	20
Total	**30**	**100**

language learning. 24 classes (80%) had teachers who discovered student misunderstanding and misconception about language learning and usage. The remaining 6 classes (20%) had teachers did not discovered student misunderstanding and misconception of language learning and usage.

Therefore, it may be mentioned that the above section on sensitivity to learners' learning attitude had three aspects: respecting diverse opinions, sensitivity to the feelings of students and identifying students' misunderstanding and misconception about language learning. It was observed that English Teachers were found to have the required levels of empathy.

Section 13: Summary of the Lesson

Summary of the Lesson

Summarised all the important points of the lesson

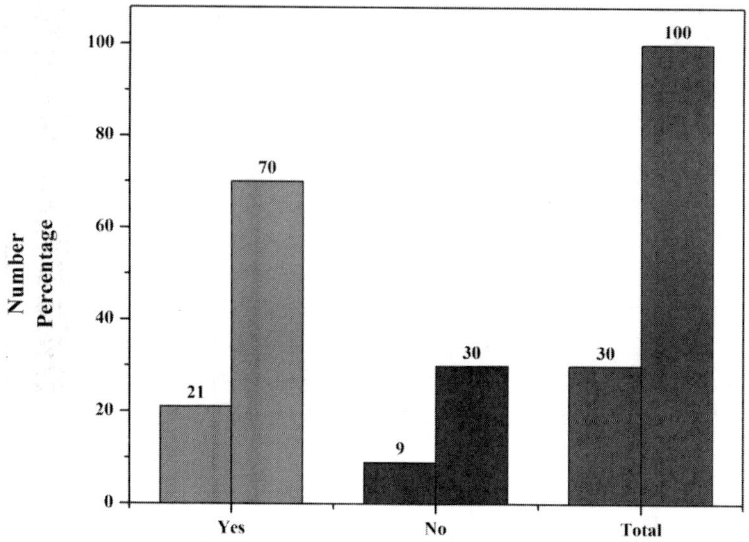

Class room observation

Classroom Observation

Number		%
Yes	21	70
No	9	30
Total	**30**	**100**

Item 13.1: This item of the Observation Schedule was intended to observe the Practicing English Teachers' are summarising all the important points of the lesson while teaching in the real classroom situation. This item was about whether the teacher summarised all the important points of the lesson. 21classes (70%) teachers had who summarised all the important points of the lesson. In the remaining 9 classes (30%) teachers did not summarize all the important points of the lesson. In conclusion, it may be mentioned that the above section on summary of the lesson has one observation related to summarising all the important points of the lesson. It was observed that among the English Teachers, 70% were able to summarise the lesson in a few words, while 30% were unable or unwilling to.

Section 14: Evaluation of Learning

There was one item in this section.

Item 14.1: This item of the Observation Schedule was intended to study if English teachers ensured learning was taking place while teaching.

This item was about whether evaluation was in place to check whether learning was taking place. Three regular classes of each English teacher had been observed that had 10 teachers with 30 classes, being observed. 24 classes (80%) had teachers who checked whether learning was taking place. The remaining 6 classes (20%) showed that evaluation was not happening at all. Therefore, it may be mentioned that the above section on evaluation of Learning contains observation related to regular evaluations to check whether learning was taking place. Observations showed that 80% of the teachers fulfilled the criteria mentioned above, while 20% did not fulfill it.

Evaluation of Learning

Evaluation was regular to check whether learning was taking place

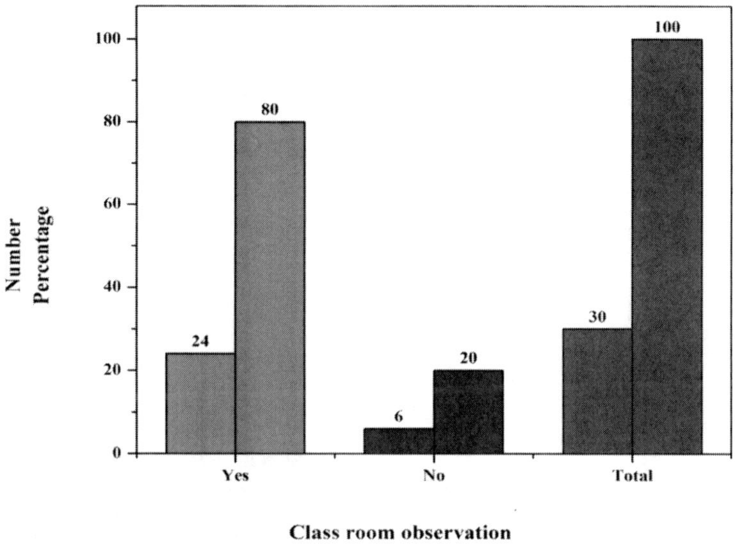

Classroom Observation

Number		%
Yes	24	80
No	6	20
Total	**30**	**100**

Section 15: Relationship of the Lesson with Future Lessons

Item 15.1: This item of the Observation Schedule was intended to observe whether English Teachers were able to relate the previous lessons with the ones that followed.

This item was about the relationship of one lesson with other lessons, whether the teacher briefly introduced the present lesson to earlier and later lessons. 8 teachers (26.67%) linked the present lesson to the earlier and later lessons. Teachers in the remaining 22 classes (73.33%) teachers failed to do it. Therefore, it may be mentioned that the above section on Relationship of the Lesson with Future Lessons contains one observation related to briefing students on earlier and later lessons. It was found that 27% fulfilled the criterion, while 73% did not.

Relationship of the Lesson with Future Lessons

Establishing the link with previous lessons as background to the new lesson

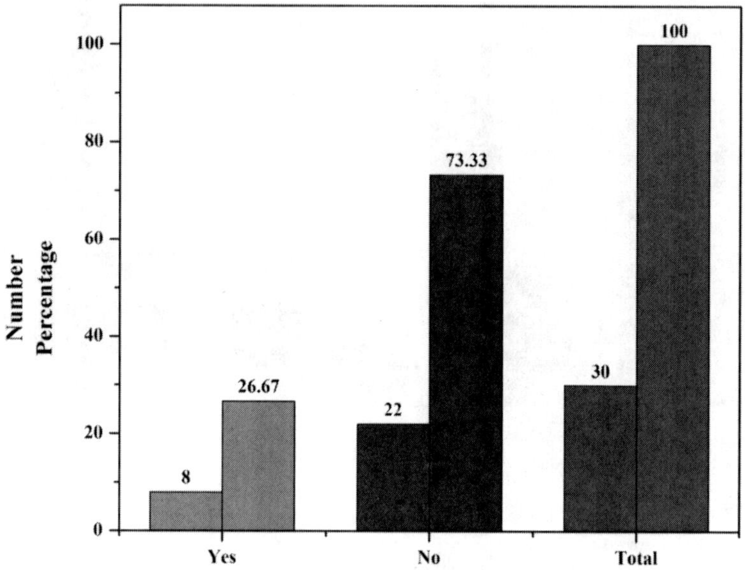

Class room observation

Classroom Observation

Number		%
Yes	8	26.67
No	22	73.33
Total	**30**	**100**

Section 16: Fulfillment of the Objectives of the Lesson

Item 16.1: This item of the Observation Schedule intended to find out of the English Teachers achieved the objectives of the lesson while teaching.

Fulfillment of the Objectives of the Lesson

The objectives of the lesson were clearly achieved

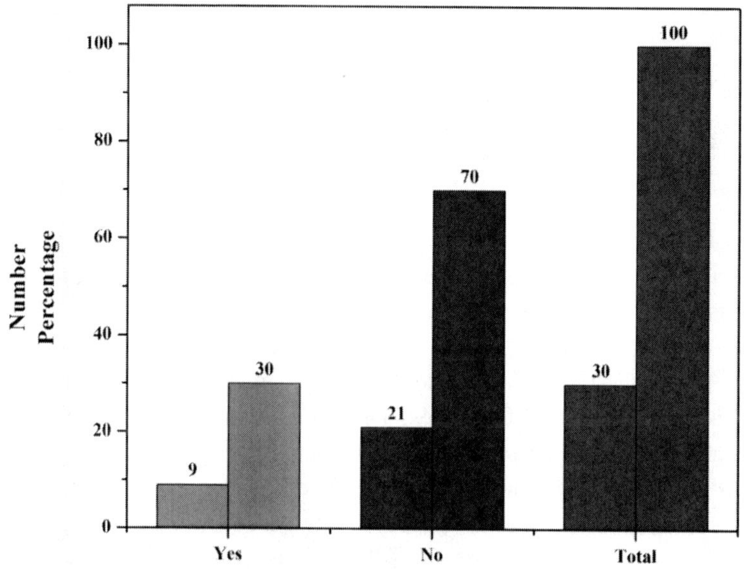

Class room observation

Classroom Observation

Number		%
Yes	9	30
No	21	70
Total	**30**	**100**

This item was about whether the objectives of the lesson were clearly achieved. Nine classes (30%) had teachers who fulfilled the objectives of the lesson; teachers who stated them achieved them too. The remaining 21 classes (70%) had teachers who failed to achieve the objectives of the lesson. Hence, it may be mentioned that the above section on Fulfillment of the Objectives of the Lesson has one aspect related to achievement of objectives of the lesson. Findings show that 30% of the teachers managed to achieve the objectives of the lesson while the remaining did not.

Qualitative Analysis of Classroom Practice

This section presents a broad description of three classes each of ten teachers. The classes were the same video recorded ones that have been described quantitatively in the previous section.

Teacher 1

Classes 1, 2 and 3

It was observed by the researcher in video recording sessions that the teacher was discussing tongue twisters and how the student can pronounce a tongue twister. He was teaching about practicing things regularly. He was using an example from the prescribed textbook about Vempati China Satyam; the various dance forms that exist in India and which dance form took its birth in AP. He gave them an assignment to pick out all the adjectives from the passage and after writing this they were asked to note down the assignment and submit it the next day.

It was observed that there are measures being employed to take into account the socio-cultural background of students. It was observed that the teacher used L1 and L2 in the classroom that was appropriate for the learners' socio-cultural background and their proficiency level. However, it may be stated that the learning in TDPs is moderately reflected in the classroom performance of the teachers with regard to curriculum, syllabus and materials development. Furthermore, it may be stated that the awareness gained from the TDPs was evident, though not so conspicuously, during teaching and preparation of supplementary materials. The training at the TDPs, as can be seen from the analysis above, had considerable impact on the methods used during classroom teaching. Though the focus of the teacher most of the time was on completing the syllabus, it may be stated that there was an endeavour undertaken by the teacher in trying to teach reading, writing, listening, speaking, grammar, vocabulary, and aspects of study skills. The teacher was not concerned about the aspect of evaluation. Furthermore, teacher-student interaction and the manner of classroom teaching reflected teacher beliefs. These inputs from the TDPs do have a bearing on teaching.

To conclude, it may be stated that the observations made through video recordings with regard to the use of tongue twisters through assignments assigned revealed the teacher's use of L1 and L2 keeping in mind the socio-cultural background and proficiency. However, the assignments submitted were disappointing. Moreover, the teacher is found to be subjective during class room interaction. Though there appeared to be an attempt to use the information learnt from TDP, evaluation and focus on research orientation was found to be lacking.

Teacher 2

Classes 1, 2 and 3

In the observation of the researcher, the teacher was found discussing a subject that dealt with the *Maestro and his mission*. It has been observed that there were instances to measures being employed to take into account the socio-cultural background of students in the class. However, the teacher was using some examples that tried to highlight socio-cultural issues. These examples were not up to the mark and though they were related to the context they were consuming time and diverting the class from teaching aspects of language and innovativeness.

The teacher is observed using translation and bilingual method in the classroom that seemed appropriate for the learners' socio-cultural background and their proficiency level. However, the methodologies learnt at the TDPs are moderately reflected in the classroom performance of the teacher with regard to curriculum, syllabus and materials development. In addition, on the other hand, the training undergone by the teachers at the TDPs appears to have had deep impact on the techniques employed by the teacher in classroom teaching. However, it was noticed that there were implicit attempts by the teacher to the teach LSRW skills, grammar, vocabulary, and study skills to students. To conclude it may be stated that the video recordings on observation reveal that there were measures employed to consider the socio-cultural background of students of the class. The examples employed in the classroom were relevant. The teacher, it is noticed, used translation and bilingual method appropriate for understanding keeping in mind learners' socio-cultural background and proficiency.

Teacher 3

Classes 1, 2 and 3

This teacher discussed a poem that was prescribed in the textbook. It is detected that there were significant attempts to take into account the socio-cultural background of the students in the classroom. Further, the teacher was employing a few examples that contextualised the poem's theme(s). The instances that were employed were related and though they were contextualised in accordance to the subject taught were taking the class from dealing the issues of language and creativity. The teacher was observed using Telugu and English in the classroom that appeared appropriate for the learners' socio-cultural background and their ability. And it was evident that the techniques and methods taught at the TDPs were seen in the classroom performance of the teacher. In addition, it has been observed that the characteristics of language teaching gained at the sessions conducted at the TDPs are reflected in the classroom, including the exercises that were undertaken by the teacher at the TDPs. Further, the teacher was thoroughly trying to make use of various techniques that he had learnt at the TDPs, while dealing with aspects of grammar, vocabulary, study skills and LSRW. Additionally, the teacher-learner conversation and the manner of classroom teaching is brought into being – reproducing the teachers' beliefs to some level. The inputs from the sessions of the TDPs do have a bearing on this. There was no reflection of the research orientation of the teacher.

To conclude, it is summarised that the teacher in question did pay attention to consider the socio-cultural background of the students. The teacher did employ a few examples that were contextualised with regard to highlighting socio-cultural aspects. The teacher has been observed using Telugu and English languages in the classroom and has shown extreme care to consider its appropriateness with regard to the learners' socio-cultural situations and ability. Moreover, the exercises that were undertaken by the teacher at the TDPs seem to have an impact in the classroom teaching. It is noticed that the teacher was trying his best to make use of various techniques that he had learnt at the TDPs – while dealing with features, viz., Grammar, Vocabulary, the aspect of Study skills and LSRW. The teacher was however not explicitly seen to be concerned with evaluation, and no reflection of the research orientation of the teacher is evident.

Teacher 4

Classes – 1, 2 and 3

It has been observed by the researcher in the video recording that the teacher was discussing characteristics of family and how the student can get an overall picture about any family. He was teaching and trying to relate various issues related to the subject matter that was being taught. He was using examples from the socio-cultural situation and trying to link them with the prescribed lesson that was being dealt with from the textbook. He was giving assignments that dealt with grammar and writing factors. It was further noticed that the teacher was using methods which were socio-culturally significant. The teacher was observed using the native language in the classroom that was appropriate for the learners' socio-cultural background. But, while using the bilingual method, the mother tongue/local language was being used most of the time rather than English.

The teacher was to an extent concerned about the facet of evaluation. Likewise, the teacher-student interaction and mode of classroom teaching was illustrated teacher beliefs. Therefore, it may be noted that the video recordings presented the teacher as teaching and relating various issues concerned with the subject matter being taught. Examples from the socio-cultural situation were linked to the prescribed lessons in the textbook. Assignments dealing with grammar and writing, methods and their employability were noticed to be socio-culturally related. The teacher is observed using the native language in the classroom appropriate to the learners' socio-cultural background. But, while using the bilingual method, the mother tongue/local language was being used more than English. In addition, the language skills received at the TDPs were demonstrated during instruction and practicing in the class. The preparation at the TDPs appears to have significant influence on the techniques employed during classroom teaching. Eventually, it is witnessed that there was an effort by the teacher while teaching skills, viz., Listening, Speaking, Reading, Writing, Grammar, Vocabulary, and the aspect of Study skills. The teacher was concerned with evaluation. The teacher-student interaction and mode of classroom teaching illustrated teacher beliefs. The techniques acquired at the TDPs did have a bearing while hardly any indication of research orientation of the teacher is noticed.

Teacher 5

Classes – 1, 2 and 3

The teacher was dealing with a prescribed lesson: *Bonsai Life* from the textbook. The teacher was motivating the students and employing various examples that were about local issues familiar to the student. He was asking them to identify the grammatical aspects from the passages of the lesson. The teacher, furthermore, was observed asking the students' questions and interacting with them. It was seen that there were initiatives to take into account the social and cultural experiences of students. Teacher was student-centered and students are actively involved in the class. The teacher used interactive and communicative language teaching techniques. Probing questions eliciting answers from the students were used.

To conclude it may be noted that the teacher was motivating and employing examples which were related to the local issues; and grammatical aspects from the passages of the lesson were given. There was teacher-student interaction and initiatives to highlight the socio-cultural issues. The teaching was of the expected standard.

Teacher 6

Classes – 1, 2 and 3

It was observed by the researcher that the teacher was discussing aspects of grammar and poetry and how the student can get an overall idea about making use of grammar in actual situations. The teacher was teaching and trying to relate various issues to the grammatical aspects that were being taught. The teacher was using examples from the local, social and cultural circumstances and trying to link them with the prescribed lesson. The teacher was making the students work on the exercises.

It was also seen that the teacher was using instances learners could relate to. The teacher was observed employing very little of L1 in the classroom. It was noticed that the insights gained at the TDPs were echoed to an extent in the classroom by the teacher with regard to supplementary materials development; she prepared language tasks using grammar rules charts, and other teaching aids in the class. In addition, the teaching of grammar and other language skills received at the TDPs were demonstrated during instruction and preparation of supplementary materials. The approach of the teacher was learner friendly, posing questions giving ample time for classroom interaction. She went beyond the text. To conclude it may be stated that the video recordings reveal that the teacher was trying to relate issues and grammatical aspects that were to be taught. The examples used were representative of the socio-cultural circumstances and linked to the lessons that were being taught. The teacher employed less of L1 in the classroom. It is noticed that the insights gained at the TDPs were echoed to an extent in the classroom by the teacher with regard to curriculum, syllabus and materials development. The teaching of grammar and other language teaching skills received at the TDPs were demonstrated during instruction and preparation of classroom teaching practice. Preparation of supplementary materials was seen. There was an effort by the teacher while teaching LSRW skills. The teacher was to an extent concerned about evaluation, but there was no evidence of research orientation of the teacher.

Teacher 7

Classes – 1, 2 and 3

It has been observed by the researcher that the teacher was discussing prescribed lesson titled *Dead Rat* and composition and how the student can get an overall idea about writing composition in actual situations. The teacher was teaching and trying to relate various issues related to aspects of interaction in day-to-day life. The teacher was using instances from the social and cultural circumstances and trying to fuse them with the lesson that was being taught from the textbook. The teacher was making the students respond in English and work on the exercises that were prescribed in the textbook.

It was noticed that the teacher was using examples and employing them which were socially and culturally related. A lot of interaction was happening in English. It was noticed that the insights gained at the TDPs were echoed to an extent in the classroom by the teacher with regard to curriculum, syllabus and materials development. To conclude, it may be stated that the teacher was focusing on the prescribed lessons and the socio-cultural circumstances were linked with interaction. The teacher was making the students communicate in English. Moreover, the insights gained at the TDPs were echoed with regard to curriculum, syllabus and materials development. It is noted that there was an effort by the teacher while teaching skills and there was focus on evaluation. The teacher-student interaction and mode of classroom teaching illustrated teacher beliefs. The abilities learnt at the TDPs did have a bearing but there was no evidence of research orientation of the teacher.

Teacher 8

Classes – 1, 2 and 3

It was observed by the researcher that the teacher was discussing aspects of grammar and poetry and how the student can get an overall idea about making use of grammar in actual situations. The teacher was teaching and trying to relate various issues related to the grammatical aspects that were being taught. The teacher was using examples from the local, social and cultural circumstances and trying to link them with the prescribed lesson that was being dealt with from the textbook. The teacher was making the students work upon the exercises that were prescribed in the textbook.

It is further noticed that the teacher was using instances and employing them which were socially and culturally related. Yet, the other abilities gained at the TDPs appear to have significant influence on the techniques employed during classroom teaching. Eventually, it has been witnessed that there was an effort carried by the teacher while teaching skills, viz., Grammar, Vocabulary, and the aspect of Study skills and less importance was given to Listening, Speaking, Reading, and Writing. The teacher was to an extent concerned about the facet of evaluation. Moreover, the teacher-student interaction and mode of classroom teaching was examined illustrating teacher beliefs to a certain level. The abilities learnt at the TDPs do have a bearing on this. There was no indication of research orientation of the teacher. To conclude, it may be mentioned that the video recordings reveal the teacher trying to relate socio-cultural issues with the grammatical aspects being taught. The teacher was using more of English and the insights gained at the TDPs were echoed in the classroom. The focus of the teacher remained mainly on the completion of the syllabus. However, the teacher was concerned about evaluation and the abilities learnt at the TDPs did appear to have a bearing while there was no evidence of research orientation of the teacher.

Teacher 9

Classes – 1, 2 and 3

It has been observed by the researcher in the video recording that the teacher was discussing about a prescribed lesson titled *Dead Rat* and composition and how the student can get an overall idea about making use of composition in actual situations. The teacher was teaching and trying to relate various issues related to the aspect of interaction in day-to-day life. The teacher was using instances from the social and cultural circumstances and trying to fuse them with the lesson that was being taught from the textbook. The teacher was making the students respond in English and work upon the exercises that were prescribed in the textbook. It is further noticed that the teacher was using instances and employing them which were socially and culturally related. The teaching of composition, speaking and other language skills received at the TDPs was reflected during instruction and preparation of teaching aids also was seen. Eventually, it has been witnessed that there was an effort made by the teacher while teaching skills, viz., Composition, Listening, Speaking, Vocabulary, and the aspect of Study skills and less importance was given to Reading and Writing. The teacher was to an extent concerned about the facet of evaluation. Moreover, the teacher-student interaction and mode of classroom teaching illustrated teacher beliefs. The abilities learnt at the TDPs do have a bearing on this. There was no indication of research orientation of the teacher noticed.

To conclude it may be summarised that the video recordings revealed the teacher discussing composition and grammar. The teacher was observed relating socio-cultural issues with the prescribed lesson. The teacher it has been further observed employed less of mother tongue in the classroom. Most of the insights learnt at the TDPs were implemented in the classroom. The language abilities gained at the TDPs by the teacher appear to have significant influence on the techniques employed during classroom teaching. The teacher appeared to be more concerned about completing the syllabus. The teacher was to an extent concerned about the evaluation and the abilities learnt at the TDPs did have a bearing. However, there was no proof of research orientation of the teacher.

Teacher 10

Classes – 1, 2 and 3

It has been observed by the researcher in the video recording, teacher was using pair work and group work in the class. The teacher was discussing aspects of grammar and poetry and how the student can get an overall idea about making use of grammar in actual situations. The teacher was teaching and trying to relate various issues related to the grammatical aspects that were being taught. Teacher taught degrees of comparisons and using metaphors like moon, comparing with beauty. Teacher was writing examples on the black board. He was checking students writing on the note books. A little correction took place in students writing. The teacher was using examples from the local, social and cultural circumstances and trying to link them with the prescribed lesson that was being dealt with from the textbook. The teacher was making the students work upon the exercises that were prescribed in the textbook. It is noticed that the insights gained at the TDPs were echoed to an extent in the classroom by the teacher with regard to materials development. Eventually, it is noticed that there was an effort carried by the instructor while teaching skills, viz., Grammar, Vocabulary, and the aspect of Study skills and less importance was given to Listening, Speaking, Reading, and Writing. The teacher was to an extent concerned about the facet of evaluating students writing. Moreover, the teacher-student interaction and mode of classroom teaching illustrated teacher beliefs to a certain level. The abilities learnt at the TDPs do have a bearing on this. There was no indication of research orientation of the teacher noticed.

It may be noted that the video recordings of the teacher demonstrate that the teacher used socio-cultural examples while teaching grammatical aspects. The teacher, it is noticed, used more of L2 in the classroom. In addition, the language abilities gained at the TDPs were employed during classroom teaching. While the teacher-student interaction and mode of classroom teaching is found illustrating teacher beliefs. The abilities learnt at the TDPs do appear to have a bearing on teacher teaching, whereas hardly any indication of research orientation of the teacher is noticed. Furthermore, it may be stated that the Resource Persons considered the aspect of sensitisation with respect to the social and cultural background of the students, viz., teachers at the TDPs. Among the respondent Practicing English Teachers, 80% felt that they were sensitised about the socio-cultural background of students, while 20% were not sure and did not properly respond to the questions asked by researcher which was reflected even in the actual classroom video recording. Subsequently, as we come to the case of issues related to the overall curriculum and syllabus content, though 90% of the Practicing English Teachers agreed that there were discussions on curriculum, syllabus and materials production at the TDPs. Moreover, the discussions at the TDPs aided their classroom teaching and the preparation of supplementary materials. Yet, it may be observed from the video recordings that not even 50% of the teachers were successful in implementing the instructions imparted at the TDPs. With respect to approaches and methods of teaching English, with reference to (listening, speaking, reading, writing, vocabulary, grammar, study skills) 80% of the teachers agreed that the TDPs raised awareness with regard to approaches and methods of teaching English. They felt that the TDPs provided training in discrete testing of the respondents, integrates testing related to testing only skill - sub-skill and skill. They opined that the traditional methods of training prove to be a waste of time and energy and instead recommended adopting practical methodology. However, 40% did not perform well in the class and were busy completing the syllabus.

Consequently, in the case of Evaluation, 90% of the responses affirmed that the TDPs discussed evaluation practices and trained teachers to evaluate more appropriately by taking feedback for every activity and involved them through reflection on teaching and learning. However, not even 10% are noticed as being successful as observed through the video recordings. Most of the teachers were found failing in the case of evaluation in the actual classroom. As the researcher takes a close look at the Teacher Beliefs and Learner Beliefs, 70% of the teachers responded that the TDPs focused on topics like teacher beliefs and learner beliefs. They felt that the discussions revealed differences in their teaching practices in their real-time classroom situation. But, nearly 50% of the teachers were found not implementing the factors in their actual classroom situation. They were more concerned about completing the syllabus. Finally, in the case of research orientation 60% of the teachers responded that the TDPs have guided and helped them in accessing library resources, journals and e-journals, to become members of Professional Bodies, aided in preparing and enabled them to develop as insightful teachers. Yet, 90% of them were not able to reflect it in their classroom teaching. They responded that reading activities helped them in classroom teaching. They further remarked that classroom interaction encouraged them to engage in research but failed to provide proper details. Subsequently, they opined that the future TDPs should have more discussions on Research awareness. However, 40% were not sure and did not properly respond to the questions asked by researcher.

5.3. In-depth analysis of classroom practices

This section presents an in-depth analysis of the classroom practices of three classes of four teachers. There are two male and two female teachers, one each from the two types of schools of APSWREIS: RPRP and Magnet schools.

Teacher 1.

The three classes dealt with:

Class 1: Maestro with a Mission

Class 2: The Bonsai Life

Class 3: The Bonsai Life

In-depth analysis Teacher 1 classroom observation

Question	Yes/ No	Example	Remarks/ Observations
(a) Are measures being employed to take into account the socio-cultural background of students?	Yes	"See! To born poor is not your mistake, but to die poor is your mistake." (class -2) "Now-a-days farmers use the plants are also grown; some certain short pattern the crop is of this size and give great fruit. We will be astonished to see them. We will be amazed to see such short trees giving great fruit" (class-2) "It's rather enough for a girl to make a washerman account. She has to be married to a man. OK! Washerman means Dhobi... In future, which girl you are going to marry? An educated girl or an illiterate girl. Which girl would you like to marry? Educated girl (students reply) so, remember it in your mind. So, don't restrict them to be at home. Be broad in your mentality. Let them go to office. Let them work." (class-3)	Based on the socio-cultural background of students, the teacher quotes Bill Gates to encourage them to work hard and succeed. The teacher brings in factors that the students relate to given their own background.
(b) Is the language used for teaching in the classroom appropriate for the learners' socio-cultural background and their proficiency level?	Yes	"Is this system followed in agriculture? Do you have any idea about it? Nowadays farmers use different plant varieties which yield a lot of fruit in a short period of time after sowing it." (class -2)	Teacher is using students' field experience and the language is pitched at the level of the students.

(c) (i) Does this learning in the teacher development programme reflect in the classroom performance of teachers with regard to curriculum, syllabus and materials development?	yes.	Has given example of a 'tongue twister' as a warm up activity. Narrated stories of Vempati Chinna Satyam (class -1) Bill Gates (class -2) Talks of kinds of agriculture. (class -3)	most of these are extra material that are given to students in the oral narrative form. They are used as warm up activities.
(ii) Does this awareness reflect during teaching and preparation of supplementary materials? Does it enable them to prepare materials independently?	Yes	Narrating stories Giving contexts	There is ample evidence of the teachers capacity to create material independently and use it in the class appropriately. These are done in the form of Narrating stories and Providing contexts for the lesson contents.
(d) Does the training at the teacher development programme impact the methods used during classroom teaching? How do they reflect in the teaching of Reading	Yes	(The teacher reads the text.) Later the teacher gives instructions like: "Now you open your books and silently read the whole thing…if you got doubts." (class—1) "You should not move your finger along with the lines. Read with your eyes okay." (class—1).	The teacher reads the lesson aloud and explains the lesson. Along with giving instructions on "Silent reading". These are important reading strategies the teacher is familiarising them with.
Writing	No	No writing task was taken up in this class	The classes observed did not have any writing task but assignments were given as homework.
Listening	No	No overt listening task	While some amount of listening is inevitable in classroom interaction, there were no overt tasks in these sessions.
Speaking	Yes	"If I say a sentence, can you repeat the same sentence?.... If you repeat the same thing again and again, it becomes easy for you". (class-2) "Can anybody say the story of Vempati Chinna Satyam from the starting in your own words? It may be wrong". (class-2)	The teacher seems to be giving ample amount of practice in speaking. This includes answering the questions, narrating the stories read and interacting with the teacher.

Grammar	No	No overt grammar task	No grammar task was overtly done during these sessions.
Vocabulary	Yes	"pick out the adjectives" (class-1) "We have come across the word *passionate*. It means......" (class 1) "*elated* means very happy and exited" (class-3)	Vocabulary tasks were taken up as part of the reading and discussion process.
Study skills	Yes	"silent reading" mentioned earlier (class 1) "now stand up and read this paragraph aloud" (class 2)	There were instances of instruction on silent reading and other study skills.
(e) Do the sessions on 'evaluation' in the teacher development programme impact the evaluation process of teachers in the classroom? How?	Yes	"Can anybody say the story of .... from the starting in your own words". (class 1)	There were instances of evaluation during the question answer sessions and the final discussions.
(f) Does the teacher-student interaction and manner of classroom teaching reflect anything on teacher beliefs? Do the inputs from the teacher development programmes have a bearing on this?	Yes	The classroom teaching reflects the teacher belief about gender sensitisation "Is your mother very busy? How does she spend her day? What does she do?" (class 2) "She makes some preparations. She sends my sister to school she cooks, she watches TV they don't want sit idle. My mother also watches TV". (class 3)	The teacher interacts with the students to make the environment student-friendly. She also attempts to raise awareness about gender in the classroom.
(g) Does class-room teaching reflect the research orientation of teachers? Are these the fallout of the teacher development programmes?	No	Nothing overt	Not overt but there is a good amount of experimentation happening in the classroom during the teaching/learning process.

This Teacher's responses in the open ended questionnaire for each section are given below (only the relevant responses have been quoted here):

Necessity of bringing in socio-cultural background

"Yes, these contexts are sometimes discussed and so teachers are also sensitised to these contexts. And these are reflected in classroom teaching."

Curriculum and syllabus

"classroom teaching can be made more effective."

"(It is important to have discussions on curriculum and syllabus). Yes, the more discussions are done the more new and innovative ideas would arise."

Appropriateness of the materials being used

"The level of language is apt to the standard of students, it would be more helpful if it is made simpler".

Approaches and methods of teaching

"TD programmes raise awareness as well as polishes the already learnt approaches and methods. They provide training to use suitable approach to the apt situations."

Evaluation

"Questioning, making students retell what is told by the teacher Quiz programmes etc."

"Yes, the evaluation is (done) more appropriately as they concentrate on making the class more child centric."

Teacher beliefs and learner beliefs

"Yes, they made us think how to make our class as innovative as possible."

Research awareness

"(Yes, they will help). If only they (research awareness programmes) are seriously implemented and practiced"

"They (Research oriented reading) helps in classroom teaching"

"Yes, they (Future TD programmes) should provide (research awareness on teaching techniques) then only there can be scope for the development of teaching techniques."

Teacher 3

The three lessons for which analysis has been provided

Class 1: Preteen Pretext

Class 2: The Treasure Within

Class 3: Grammar

Question	Yes/ No	Example	Remarks
(a) Are measures being employed to take into account the socio-cultural background of students?	Yes	"In ancient days information transfer from one place to another place HOW? Through letters from letters now we got information how? Through the cell phones. We sent the message writing the few words and sending the message. Today we discuss about the cell phones. Preteen Pretext What do you see in the picture? Mother is sitting in the sofa. Daughter is sitting in the chair upstairs." (class 1)	The teacher reflected on the socio-cultural background of the students. Teacher is trying to differentiate between old form of communication (snail mail) and modern form of communication (electronic mail). The language of the Teacher however, has serious flaws and can even impede understanding at times.
(b) Is the language used for teaching in the classroom appropriate for the learners' socio-cultural background and their proficiency level?	No	"If we permit the cell phone to the class. You don't listen to the class. You always play with phones."	There is no overt attempt to simplify the language of the text. But simpler examples are given to make the text comprehensible.
(c) (i) Does this learning in the teacher development programme reflect in the classroom performance of teachers with regard to curriculum, syllabus and materials development?	No	No. There is not attempt to create overt supplementary material but the lessons have been contextualised. "When my daughter goes outside, immediately, I check where she was how?"	In a very limited way, there is attempt to contextualise the material, give relevant references and supplement the given text.
(ii) Does this awareness reflect during teaching and preparation of supplementary materials? Does it enable them to prepare materials independently?	No	Used only Text No other materials	Used black board and lecture method
(d) Does the training at the teacher development programme impact the methods used during classroom teaching? How do they reflect in the teaching of Reading,	Yes	Teacher asked students to read aloud the meaning on the board "read the meanings of... on the board" (class-2)	Teacher asks students to read aloud the vocabulary items put up on the board

Writing	No	There were no writing tasks given during the classes observed for this teacher	No writing tasks given during the during the classes observed.
Listening	No	No. The teacher did not give time to test the listening comprehension of students.	No overt task was given but it was assumed that listening comprehension would be activated during teaching.
Speaking	No	No speaking activity	The teacher did not include any speaking activity in the classes observed.
Grammar	Yes	"Today we discuss about Parts of Speech. Every language has to write some rules and conditions. Words are divided into 8 kinds. According to their functions are called parts of speech. Noun Pronoun Verb Adverb Adjective Preposition Conjunction Interjection" (class-3)	This teacher gave a lot of importance to teaching grammar. There were problems however in the teacher's usage of English.
Vocabulary	Yes	Look at rhyming words in the Poem Phone – alone Night—light Rage—page...(class-1)	Teacher taught voca-bulary using rhyming words in the poem.
Study skills	No	No overt teaching of study skills.	The teacher did not spend time to overtly teach the study skills
(e) Do the sessions on 'evaluation' in the teacher development programme impact the evaluation process of teachers in the classroom? How?	No	No Evaluation was done during the classes observed.	This teacher hardly included any evaluation component in her teaching. There were sporadic questions asked but she did not wait for students to respond.

(f) Does the teacher-student interaction and manner of classroom teaching reflect anything on teacher beliefs? Do the inputs from the teacher development programmes have a bearing on this?	Yes.	The teacher believes that technology is a hindrance for the learners. "Mother says do homework but her child did not listen. ....the child goes with friends through the cellphones" She called to her daughter. No doubt cell phone is easy but no face to face"	The teacher beliefs about the hindering role of cell phones is reflected in the talk in class.
(g) Does class-room teaching reflect the research orientation of teachers? Are these the fallout of the teacher development programmes?	No	Nothing overt	No. There is no apparent sign of orientation. The teacher made no attempt to try new methods or teaching processes in the classroom.

Teacher responses in the open ended questionnaire

Necessity of bringing in socio-cultural background

"Yes, I believe that such inputs (aids) would have a bearing which teaching in my class to see the child to develop memory."

Curriculum and syllabus

"Different aspects are discussed in these programmes (presentations-practice-production-describing things)"

Teacher beliefs and learner beliefs

"Yes, I implement these discussion difference aspects LSRW skills in classroom teaching."

Teacher 4

The three lessons for which analysis has been provided

Class 1: The Tattered Blanket

Class 2: I Can Take Care of Myself

Class 3: The Bonsai Life

Question	Yes/ No	Examples	Remarks
(a) Are measures being employed to take into account the socio-cultural background of students?	Yes	"(We have)Economic problems for that no joint families reasons. ....Economic and social causes also affect joint families. Now we are going to read about the present day situations about the families. Families are not joint family's only nuclear families. Nuclear families in the sense, father, mother and two children (students) today we find many nuclear families." (class-1) "The mother rat decided to marry her daughter. Generally when parents decide to marry their children they look for grooms, village to village." (class-2) "Village life and city life two life styles are there. Which life style do you like most. Village life – peaceful place, fresh air, pollution free. City life – pollution, busy life, air pollution, no. of vehicles moving here and there. That's why pollution, etc. so, you don't like city life only you like village life." (class-3)	Teacher is relating modern family system in the society. Teacher is explaining the general approach of parents towards a search of groom for their daughter. Teacher compares city life and village life, by carefully drawing attention of the students to environmental issues.
(b) Is the language used for teaching in the classroom appropriate for the learners' socio-cultural background and their proficiency level?	Yes	"Why are you not asking Vimala ...text...Gopi's name is Vimala. Nuvvu busy gaunnavu, marivimala, ni kids niaaina letter wrayamaniadagavachukada. (you are busy. At least you can ask the kids to write a letter)" (class-1) "general ga pelli cheyalanukunnapudu evaraina dhanavantudiki, gunavantudiki iwalanukuntaru." (everyone would like to marry their daughters to rich and talented people with good character) (class-2)	Teacher uses bilingual method to facilitate students to comprehend theme of lesson.

(c) (i) Does this learning in the teacher development programme reflect in the classroom performance of teachers with regard to curriculum, syllabus and materials development?	Yes	No supplementary materials used in the class. But the teacher is making extensive use of bilingualism and provided contexts for the students to think about.	The teacher did not provide any supplementary material but gave extended context to help comprehension.
(ii) Does this awareness reflect during teaching and preparation of supplementary materials? Does it enable them to prepare materials independently?	Yes	There is no evidence of any ability to prepare formal supplementary material. But extensive bilingual material has been provided almost as a parallel text.	The teacher has been able to provide oral narratives in the home language of the students. This can be thought of as an ability to make new material.
(d) Does the training at the teacher development programme impact the methods used during classroom teaching? How do they reflect in the teaching of Reading	Yes	"See the picture and answer the question that follows 1. What do you observe? Two families. Nuclear family, Joint family. 2. Do we find many joint families in our society? Yes/ No? Give reasons. No there are joint families. But there are not many joint families, in the society." "What are the reasons?" (class-1)	Teacher used pre-reading task teaching the lesson :*The tattered Blanket.* teacher introduced the author Kamala Das.
Writing	No	No overt writing task was given	The teacher did not provide any overt writing task during the sessions observed.
Listening	Yes	The teacher provides alternative narratives and asks questions on them "What do you think the most important thing to learn live well" (class-1) "What are the qualities that you have to be independent in your life?" (class-1)	The teacher has asked questions on the narratives. This would involve a good amount of listening comprehension.
Speaking	Yes	Questions asked and discussed on the narratives provided "Answer the questions now" "Do you agree or Disagree? Why?" (class-1)	Although no extensive speaking activity has been included, the teacher seems to have attempted to involve the students in discussion.

Grammar	No	On toes means busy, move on. On toes is also a phrase. I am always busy. Last year promotion Why are you not asking Vimala …text…Gopi's name is Vimala. Nuvvu busy ga unnavu, mari vimala, ni kids niaaina letter wrayamani adaga vachukada.(class-1)	Teacher uses situational approach while teaching grammar.
Vocabulary		Tattered means torn exasperatingly = angrily.	Meanings are given directly. No overt vocabulary tasks are done.
Study skills	Yes	Teacher made tables on the board and asked students to provide information.	Teacher seems to be focusing on information transfer and even enabling the students to make inferences on the basis of diagrams. The teacher also provided a pre-reading activity and engaged the class using the bilingual method.
(e) Do the sessions on 'evaluation' in the teacher development programme impact the evaluation process of teachers in the classroom? How?	Yes	"1. The narrator receives letter very frequently True sir 2. The letter brought the news of the narrator's sister and brother-in-law arrival. True sir 3. The narrator's husband was very happy to hear the news of the visitors. True sir 4. Akkayya was not interested to continue her studies. False (teacher : In those days girl education is not important) 5. The narrator's husband likes the traditional food of Andhra Pradesh? True sir"(class-3).	There were instances of evaluation during the question answer sessions and the final discussions.

(f) Does the teacher-student interaction and manner of classroom teaching reflect anything on teacher beliefs? Do the inputs from the teacher development programmes have a bearing on this?	Yes	"Answer the questions now: 1. What do you think the most important thing to learn live well. Ans: how to protect myself and become strong. 2. What are the qualities that you have to be independent in your life. Ans: Job, goal reach, target reach (students) hardworking. 3. Do you agree or disagree with the daughter rat? Disagree? No sir Agree"	The teacher interacts with the students to motivate
(g) Does class-room teaching reflect the research orientation of teachers? Are these the fallout of the teacher development programmes?	Yes	The teacher's use of bilingual narratives reflects on the research orientation of the teacher.	The teachers use of the bilingual method as a pre-task is a distinct research orientation. Probably, it is the teacher's attempt to mediate the learning in the given text.

Teacher responses in the open ended questionnaire:

Curriculum and syllabus

"It (the TDP) enriched my C.R. teaching"

"Yes, A.V. Aids, charts, skits, etc. these materials create interest in learning among the students"

Appropriateness of the materials being used

(The materials used in the programmes were) very good.

(The materials used in the programmes were) up to the level of their (the pupils)

Understanding

Approaches and methods of teaching

"Classroom teaching become very easy task. It's now student centered."

Evaluation

"(I used) bilingual method for evaluation.

Action research

"It helps to know the latest techniques of teaching. It helps to update ourselves."

Teacher 9

The three lessons for which analysis has been provided

Class 1: The Dead Rat

Class 2: The Dead Rat

Class 3: The Dead Rat

Question	Yes/ No	Examples	Remarks
(a) Are measures being employed to take into account the socio-cultural background of students?	Yes	"It means a person who has no home and no job ...keeps roaming... generally we see such people also. They don't study properly. They don't do any kind of job. Simply they want to eat, watch TV, go around with friends and half of their life is only like this gone..." (class-1) "If the child is there, father is not there. Father is dead only mother is there, what the mother will think" (class-1)	The teacher does not give any exclusive context to create the background but weaves it often into the teaching of the lesson.
(b) Is the language used for teaching in the classroom appropriate for the learners' socio-cultural background and their proficiency level?	Yes	Teacher: you take some money and what you have to do? Students: business Teacher: take up our business and then Students: pay Teacher: repay the money, return the money, ok, or you keep the without paying? Students: no madam Teacher: you have to return? Students: yes	Carefully elicited responses from their experiences. The teacher also seems to be making the material appropriate to their proficiency level.

(c) (i) Does this learning in the teacher development programme reflect in the classroom performance of teachers with regard to curriculum, syllabus and materials development?	Yes	The teacher modifies the teaching material as and when the teaching is going on-	Although there is no evidence of preparation of material, the teacher seems to be contextualising the lessons and making it richer than the given text.
(ii) Does this awareness reflect during teaching and preparation of supplementary materials? Does it enable them to prepare materials independently?	No	No supplementary material was overtly made or used in the class	Although no supplementary material was overtly used, the teacher attempted to sufficiently supplement the lesson by extended examples and discussions.
(d) Does the training at the teacher development programme impact the methods used during classroom teaching? How do they reflect in the teaching of Reading.	Yes	The teacher initiates a reading task at the beginning by eliciting responses " find the picture on the page and list out the different things"	The teacher seems to be engaging the students in a close reading task. This can be thought of as a pre reading activity given before the teaching of the lesson.
Writing	No	No writing activity given	No writing activity given during the classes observed.
Listening	No	No overt listening activity	No overt listening activity but the interactive nature of the class assumes the necessity of intense listening and responding.
Speaking	Yes	"Tell me whatever you find in that picture". (class-1) "everyone is talking about something. What are they talking about? Tell me" (class-1) " Did you understand anything from this para? ...you want to speak out once again?"(class-2s)	The teacher seems to continuously involve the students in speaking activities drawn from both the lesson being taught and the supplementary examples the teacher provides. Most of the speaking tasks emphasise the teacher's need to enable the students mediate between the lesson and their own experience.

Grammar	No	No grammar tasks undertaken	No grammar task was undertaken during the classes observed. This was probably because of the flow the teacher wanted to sustain.
Vocabulary	Yes	"So, vagabond, vagabond is a new word here just you refer your dictionary, just open a dictionary and see, just go through" " it means a person who has no home and who has no job, so he moves away from one particular place to another place, he continuously keeps on roaming without any home without any job that kind of person is called as a vagabond"	The teacher seems to discuss the difficult words in the text by contextualising them and by providing extended contexts for them. This can be seen as an effort to inculcate inferencing abilities in students.
Study skills	Yes	The teacher engaged the students in activities like using a dictionary, guessing meaning, etc.	The teacher seems to be extensively using study skills, prompting the students to come up with responses and understand the content independently in different ways.
(e) Do the sessions on 'evaluation' in the teacher development programme impact the evaluation process of teachers in the classroom? How?	Yes	"Teacher: sit down, next what is the meaning of this, one day Madananka absconded from his house, absconded, do you know the meaning? Students: escape Teacher: one girl, one girl Students: sneak quickly and secretly Teacher: sneak quickly and secretly, secretly means, secretly doing something what is the meaning of that? Students: telling Teacher: keep telling Students: no	Teacher is assessing students' listening by interactive mode.

		Teacher: then what is the meaning of that? You may tell to your friend that is secret. Secret means what? Students: personally"	
(f) Does the teacher-student interaction and manner of classroom teaching reflect anything on teacher beliefs? Do the inputs from the teacher development programmes have a bearing on this?	Yes	Teacher: Ok, children for today, you turn the page 139, you find the picture on that page, just you have to list out what are the different things in that picture, one by one you tell me whatever you find in that picture… yes we will start. Students: House Teacher: You can see a house, then what else Students: Rat Teacher: You can see rats, Students: One boy	The teaching process demonstrates the teachers' beliefs about engaging with the students, mediating the learning process, etc.
(g) Does class-room teaching reflect the research orientation of teachers? Are these the fallout of the teacher development programmes?	Yes	The teaching session shows the teacher experimenting and trying different ways of making students interpret, read, respond and understand.	Not overt but there is a good amount of experimentation happening in the classroom during the teaching /learning process. Mediation is one of chief methods of experimentation taken up in the classes of this teacher.

Teacher responses in the open ended questionnaire:

Necessity of bringing in socio-cultural background

"Generally, teachers are rarely sensitised regarding the socio-cultural background of the students."

"it is essential as the teacher will come to know about the social and cultural background of the learners and deal with them accordingly."

Curriculum and syllabus

"These discussions provide us for deeper understanding of the text and give more illustrations to explain the context clearly."

Appropriateness of the materials being used

"The learners can relate the text to their real-life situations."

"Teacher Development Programmes seldom provide any training to independently create new material"

Approaches and methods of teaching

"The training of dealing with CCE texts has helped a lot when I tried it out in my class my students were able to frame many sentences on their own when the cover picture was exploited"

Evaluation

"Yes, the TD programmes discuss evaluation practices and give idea of observation and various methods of evaluation tools."

Teacher beliefs and learner beliefs

"Yes, the future TD programmes should have more of such discussions."

This section makes an in-depth analysis of the classes of four teachers. The analysis shows that the teachers are aware of the benefits of the teacher training programme and want to incorporate their learning in their classes. However, we find that sometimes it is done overtly but most of the times the method used or the research orientation seems to be reflected in their teaching process. Probably, more intense training would help them develop these teaching /learning aspects and implement them in the classroom more effectively.

Chapter - 6

Effectiveness of Teacher Development Programmes for English Teachers

We have attempted to find the effectiveness of TDPs for English teachers of Social Welfare Residential Schools in the States of Andhra Pradesh and Telangana. It is an exploratory case study using a mixed methods approach. This study has two research questions, given below. The research questions and tools used to collect data for the research questions were as follows:

Question 1: Do the objectives of TDPs match with the needs and expectations of the teachers (with specific reference to the English component) of APSWREIS? Tools Include (a) Questionnaire for academic coordinator, (b) Semi-structured interviews for resource persons, (c) Questionnaire for teachers (closed-ended), (d) Questionnaire for teachers Questionnaire (Open-ended), and (e) Observation of TDPs.

Question 2: Are the teachers' views and learning reflected in actual classroom practice? Tools include (a) Observation checklist—quantitative, and (b) Observation checklist—qualitative.

The research tools used for the study provided some valuable information concerning English teachers' teaching abilities. The effectiveness of TDPs for teachers was recorded after their attending the TDPs which aimed at improving their teaching skills. In this chapter, the findings of the study are presented along with discussions on the findings, the implications of the study, suggestions for further research and limitations of the study. Using the data collected through quantitative and qualitative methods, the study attempted to find answers to the research questions proposed. The findings of the study are presented below in the form of answers to the research questions. Based on the data collected and the conclusions drawn from each of the tools, it was found that there was a good amount of match between the objectives of the TDPs and the needs and expectations of the teachers of APSWREIS. The teachers' responses to the questionnaires shows that they were aware of the benefits drawn from TD Programmes. The findings from the study confirmed that the secondary school teachers are able to modify, improve, draw from the TDPs made available to them. The study also shows that they use the information given in these programmes in many innovative ways during these classrooms. Some of them are, viz., Mediating the teaching through social and cultural contexts and extended examples, Use of bilingualism to make the teaching learning process more accessible to learners, and using testing for the purpose of teaching and continually evaluating the learning process.

The analysis shows that the teachers' views are largely reflected in the classroom teaching practices. Largely they use reading and speaking, listening, study skills, vocabulary learning very innovatively in the class room context and expressed the views in the open-ended questionnaire. Examples of this can be extensively found in in-depth analysis of the four teachers responses provided in the chapter 5. On the whole the analysis shows that TDPs had significant impact on the teacher beliefs, teaching methodologies and their understanding of the evaluation procedures. One can conclude from this the more rigorous implementation of the TDPs can have significant impact on teachers in the secondary level.

The above-mentioned findings point to some interesting propositions and indicate that institutional responsibility plays a major role in designing effective teacher development programmes. While trying to envisage a teacher development programme, the objectives of the Society, the needs of the participating teachers, and the objectives of the TDPs must coincide with one another. Especially the resource persons must be aware of the specific objectives of the TDPs. Only then, the teachers would improve as desired by the Society. It is a well-known fact that effectiveness of teacher development is a continuous process. Therefore, follow-up programmes must be designed and the teachers' classroom practices must be recorded periodically and future TDPs should be designed accordingly to plug the lacunae in pedagogic practices of the teachers.

We have examined only in the Social welfare schools of Andhra Pradesh and Telangana, it can be done with tribal welfare schools of Andhra Pradesh and Telangana or some other state. Secondly, a study can be conducted on the follow-up programmes at the schools of participating teachers. Thirdly, the policy perspectives on teacher development programme in Andhra Pradesh or elsewhere can be looked into. Finally, further research can be done on teacher beliefs of English language teachers. It is strongly felt that no matter how much we spend or the pains the resource persons and administration take in conducting the TDPs, if the teachers do not have positive belief regarding TDPs all our efforts will go in vain.

Bibliography

Agnihotri, R. K., & Khanna, A. L. (Eds.). (1995). *English language teaching in India: issues and innovations* (Vol. 2). New Delhi: SAGE.

Agnihotri, R.K. and A.L Khanna (1992). *Issues and Options in Language Teaching*. New Delhi: SAGE.

Ahmad Faiyaz, S.(1994). "*Towards Incorporating a study skills component in teacher training programmes at the tertiary level.*" Unpublished M.phil. Dissertation. Hyderabad: CIEFL.

Akinyemi Akintunde (2005). *Integrating culture and second language teaching through Yoruba personal names. The Modern Language Journal* Vol. 89. pp. 115- 125.

Allwright, D., Allwright, R., & Bailey, K. M. (1991). *Focus on the language classroom: An Introduction to Classroom Research for Language Teachers*. Cambridge University Press.

Allwright, Dickm, Kathleen M. Bailey (1990). *Focus on the Language Classroom*. London: CUP.

Al-Mutawa Najat & Suad Al-Furaih. (2005). Evaluation of the In-Service Education and Training Programme for Kuwait Army Instructors. *Journal of In-Service Education.* Vol. 31, No. 2, pp. 373-391.

Amritavalli, R. (2007). *English in Deprived Circumstances Maximizing Learner Autonomy*. New Delhi: Cambridge University Press.

An Anthology. (2005). *ELT World-A bird's Eye view*. (English language teaching, Teacher and Trainer Training and Development.) R.I.E. South India.

Ananthakrishnan. (1995). 'Dairy Study as a Tool for Teachers.' In the Language Curriculum: Dynamics of change, Vol. 2 *Teacher as Researcher* (eds.)

Anderson, Jason. (2007). *Teamwork Interactive tasks to get students talking*: New Delhi. CIEFL Hyderabad -7.

Anderson, J.Neil. (2003). Metacognitive Reading Strategies Increase L2 Performance. *The Language teacher.* Vol. 27, No. 7, pp. 20-23.

Ashman, F. Adrian and Robert N.F. Conway (1989). *Cognitive strategies for special education.* London and New York: Routledge.

Aslam Mohammad. (1999). Teacher development and communicative language teaching. English studies in India. A *Journal of Litt. Language.* Vol. VII, pp. 60-71.

Aziz, Arfah Abdul (1981). *Strategies for Communication between Teachers and Pupils in a Rural Malaysian School*. Singapore: Singapore University Press.

Bailey, K. M. (1990). '*The use of diary studies in teacher education programmers'* in

Baker Joanna and Heather Westrup. (2006). *The English Language Teacher's Handbook: How to teach Large Classes with few Resources*. London: Continuum.

Baxter, P., & Jack, S. (2008). Qualitative case study methodology: Study design and implementation for novice researchers. *The qualitative report, 13*(4), 544-559.

Beck, Angela. (2002). Writing Strategies Worksheet. *TESOL Journal*. Vol. 11, No. 1.

Becktold Toni Hill. (2001). Brain based Instruction in Correctional Settings: Strategies for Teachers. *Journal of Correctional Education*. Vol. 52, No. 3, pp. 95-97.

Begum, Zohra. (1960). Suggestions for the improvement of seminars and workshops. *Teacher Education*. Vol. IV, No. 4, pp. 41.

Berger Jennifer Garvey, Katherine C.Boles & Vivian Troen.(2005). Teacher research and school change: paradoxes, problems, and possibilities. *Teaching and Teacher Education*. Vol. 21, pp. 93-105.

Bhakat, C Hitesh (2005). Peer teaching –A tool for reflective teacher. *ELT news* Vol. 4, No. 3, pp. 19-26.

Bharathi, T.S. (1995). *The role of teacher development in the Effectiveness of language curriculum reform*. Unpublished M.phil. Dissertation. Hyderabad: CIEFL.

Bhasin, Veena.(1996). The changing focus in teacher preparation. In Rama Mathew and R.L. Eapen (eds), *The language curriculum: Dynamics of change*. Hyderabad: CIEFL. pp. 33-36.

Billows, F. L. & Dr A.S.N.Pillai. (1957). Psychology for teachers of English. Vol. 4, No. 3, pp. 62-66.

Block, David. (2004).Globalisation and language teaching. *ELT Journal*. Vol. 58/1, Oxford University Press.

Bloomer, Aileen, Patrick Griffiths and Andrew John Merrison. (2005). *Introducing Language in Use – A Course Book*. Routledge: London.

Bloomer, Aileen, Patrick Griffiths and Andrew John Merrison. (2005). *Introducing Language in Use*. Routledge: London.

Boon, Andrew. (2003). *On the road to teacher development: Awareness, discovery, and Action. The language teacher:* Vol. 27, No. 12.

Boon, Andrew (2003). *On the Telephone. Designing Materials to Enhance Learner Listening Strategies on the Telephone. Modern English Teacher*. Vol. 15, No. 3, pp. 26-33.

Borg, Michaela. (2001). Teachers' beliefs. *ELT Journal,* Vol. 55/2, No. 186-183.

Borg, Simon. (1998). Data-based teacher development. *ELT Journal*. Vol. 52/4, pp. 273-281.

Breen, M. (1989). The evaluation cycle for language learning tasks. *The second language curriculum, 187206*.

Brookhart, M. Susan. (1990). Empirical evidence that school-university collaboration is multicultural education. *Teaching& teacher education*. Vol. 6, No. 2, pp. 149-163.

Brown, A. Robert (2005). Autonomous learning strategies of Japanese EFL students. *The Language teacher.* Vol. 29, No. 4, pp. 11-14.

Brown, G. (1995). *Dimensions of difficulty in listening comprehension.* In D. J. Mendelsohn Brown, H. D. (1994). *Teaching by principles: An interactive approach to language pedagogy.* Englewood Cliffs, New Jersey: Prentice Hall Regents. 416.

Bruton, Anthony. (1984). *Language learning strategies: a case study. Modern English Teacher.* Vol. 12, No. 2, pp. 9-11.

Buckby, Michael.(1979). Twenty ways to use flashcards part 2, *Modern English Teacher.* Vol. 7, No. 1/4, pp. 22-23.

Burns, Chris. (2005). Tensions between national, school and needs: a survey of teachers' views about continuing professional development within a group of rural primary school. *Journal of in- service education.* Vol. 31, No. 2, pp. 353-371.

Byram, M., & Feng, A. (2004). Culture and language learning: Teaching, research and scholarship. *Language teaching, 37*(3), 149-168.

CBSE-*ELT Curriculam Implementation Study (1993-97) Final Report 1997.* Unpublished Hyderabad: CIEFL.

Celce-Murcia Marianne. (1993). The Rile of Strategies in Language Teaching. *TESOL Quarterly.* Vol. 37, No. 1, pp. 119-120.

Chambers, G. (1996). Listening, Why? How? *Language Learning Journal, 4, 23-7. change*. Hyderabad. Orient Longman.

Chandler, Jon and Mark Stone. (2004). The Resourceful English teacher. A complete teaching companion. New Delhi. Viva Books Private Limited.

Cheung, Chi-kim. (2001). The use of popular culture as motivates students. *ELT Journal,* Vol. 55, No. 1, pp. 55-61.

CIEFL. (1994). *Teacher as Researcher*, CBSE- ELT curriculum implementation study (A CIEFL-CBSE joint project). Hyderabad: CIEFL.

Clarke, Alan. (2004). *E-Learning skills*. New York. Palagrave Macmillan.

Clarlson, Jean. (2005). Reformation of the Macedonian teacher education programme. *Educational Research,* Vol. 47, No. 3, pp. 319.

Clennell, Charles. (1994). Investigating the Use of Communication Strategies by Adult Second Language Learners: A Case for Trusting Your Own Judgment in Classroom Research. *Tesol Journal,* Vol. 4, No. 1, pp. 32-35.

Cook, V. (2001). *Second language learning and language teaching*. London: Edwin Arnold. Corwin Press.

Crandall, J. J. (2000). Language teacher education. *Annual review of applied linguistics*, *20*, 34-55.

Crookall, David. (1983). *Learner training: a neglected strategy-Part 1. Modern English Teacher.* Vol. 11, No. 1, pp. 41-43.

Crookall, David. (1983). Learning Training: a neglected Strategy. *Modern English Teaching,* Vol. 11.1, No. 1, pp. 41-42.

Cullinan, E. (1992). Whole language and children's literature. *Language Arts.* Vol. 69, pp. 426-430.

Das, K.Bikram (1975). Educational Television in the Indian Context- A Language Teaching Point of View. *CIEFL Bulletin.* Vol. 11, pp. 73-82.

Day, Christopher (1987). 'Professional learning through collaborative in-service activity.' In John Smyth (ed), *Educating teachers: Changing the nature of pedagogical knowledge.* London: The Falmer Press Dennis.

Donaghue Helen. (2002). An instrument to elicit teachers' beliefs and assumptions. *English language teaching Journal,* Vol. 57, No. 4, pp. 344-349.

Dörnyei, Z., & Taguchi, T. (2009). *Questionnaires in second language research: Construction, administration, and processing.* Routledge.

Douglas, W. Jack and Victoria C. Stage. (2005). *Success strategies for Expats.* Training and development. September 2005. pp. 48-52.

Duff, P. A. (2007). *Second language socialisation as sociocultural theory: Insights and issues. Language teaching, 40(4),* 309-319.

Durga, Bhavani, K. (2007). Teacher and learner empowerment in the widening context of teaching English as a global language. *The Indian Journal of English studies.* Vol. XLIV, pp. 244-255.

Ehrman, M., & Oxford, R. (1990). Adult language learning styles and strategies in an intensive training setting. *The modern language journal, 74*(3), 311-327.

Elaine, C. Stephens and Jean E. Brown.(2001). A Handbook of content literacy strategies: 75 practical reading and writing ideas. *TESOL Journal 44-45.*

Ellis D James. (1992). *Teacher Development in Advanced Educational Technology. Journal of Science Education and Technology.* Vol. 1, No. 1, pp. 49-65.

Ellis Gail and Barbara Sinclair. (1989). Learning to learn English: A course in learner training. *TESOL Quarterly* Vol. 37, No. 1, pp. 122.

Ellis, N. C., & Laporte, N. (1997). *Contexts of acquisition: Effects of formal instruction and naturalistic exposure on second language acquisition. Tutorials in bilingualism: Psycholinguistic perspectives, 53-83.*

Ellis, R. (1995). *The Study of Second Language Acquisition***.** Oxford: Oxford University.

Ellis, R. (2003). *Task – Based Language Teaching and Learning.* Oxford: Oxford University Press.

Evmorfia Panourgia Mr. & Dr Sylvester S.P. (2006). Learning and Teaching strategies in second language learning. *ELT News.* Vol. 5, No. 3, pp. 17-22.

Fang, Zhihui. (1996). A review of research on teacher beliefs and practices. *Educational Research Journal.* Vol. 38, No. 1, pp. 47-65.

Feldman, A. Daniel Ph.D. *Critical thinking Strategies for decision making.* New Delhi. CIEFL Hyderabad-7

Feng, Xiwu. (1998). Reading easy and difficult texts in English and Chinese: strategy use by native speakers of Chinese. *Asian Journal of English language teaching.* Vol. 8, pp. 19-40.

Field, John. (1998). Skills and strategies: towards a new methodology for listening. *ELT Journal.* Vol. 52/2, pp. 110-118.

Flowerdew, John and Lindsay Miller. (1996). Lecturer perceptions, problems and strategies in second language lecturers. *RELC Journal.* Vol. 27, No. 1, pp. 23.

Flowerdew John, Lindsy Miller and David C S LI. (2000). Chinese lecturers' perceptions, problems and strategies in lecturing to Chinese- speaking students. *Regional Language centre Journal.* Vol. 31, No. 1, pp.

Flowerdew, Lynne. (1997). Interpersonal Strategies: Investigating Interlanguage corpora. *Regional Language centre* Vol. 28, No. 1, pp. 72-73.

Flowerdew, J. (1998). Language learning experience in L2 teacher education. *TESOL Quarterly, 32*(3), 529-536.

Flurkey, D. Alan and Richard J. Meyer (eds) (1994). *Under the Whole Language Umbrella-Many Cultures, Many Voices.* United States of America: National Council of Teachers of English.

Freeman, Donald and Jack C. Richards.(1996). *Language Teaching Research,* Vol. 1, No. 1, pp. 81-92.

Freeman, D. and J.C. Richard (eds.). (1996). *Teacher in the Language Teaching.* Cambridge: Cambridge University Press.

Freeman, E. David. & Yvonne S.Freeman.(1993). *Strategies for promoting the primary languages of all students. The Reading Teacher.* Vol. 46, No. 7, pp. 552-558.

Fu Gail, Schaefer. (1998). Teaching by principles: An interactive approach to language pedagogy. *Asian Journal of English language teaching.* Vol. 8, pp. 117-123.

Fung, Yvonne. (2000). A Constructive Strategy for Developing Teachers for Change: a Hong Kong experience. *Journal of In-Service Education.* Vol. 26, No. 1, pp. 153-167.

Gadkar, Vineeta. C. (1977). *"An experiment in designing a need-based media training kit for English language teachers."* Unpublished M.Litt. dissertation. Hyderabad: CIEFL.

Gareth, Morgan. (1983). *Beyond method Strategies for Social research.* Sage publications, Beverly Hills /London /New Delhi.

Garies, Elisabeth.(2005). Vocabulary strategy Work for advanced learners of English. *English teaching Forum.* Vol. 43, No. 2, pp. 24-35.

George, P.T. (1982). Teaching English to the Disadvantaged Sections of the Community- towards the development of a Curricular Strategy. *CIEFL Bulletin.* Vol. XVIII, No. 1 & 2, pp. 53-68.

Goh, C. M Christine.(2002). Learners' self-reporters on comprehension and learning strategies for listening. *Asian Journal of English language teaching.* Vol. 12, pp. 45-67.

Gohil, Surendrasinh. (2006). ICT Tools and competencies for teacher for teacher education. *ELT News,* Vol. 1:5, No. 1&2, pp. 51-62.

Goodman, S. Keeneth. (1992). I didn't found whole language. *The reading teacher.* Vol. 46, No. 3, pp. 188-199.

Graham, G Janet. (1999). Four Strategies to Improve the Speech of Adult Learners. *TESOL journal,* Vol. 3, No. 3, pp. 26-28.

Graham, M. P. (1989). Language learning strategies: *TESOL Quarterly,* Vol. 37, No. 1, pp. 121.

Griffee, T. D. (2012). An Introduction To Second Language Research Method. *TESL-EJ Publications*.

Griffiths, Carol and Judy M. parr. (2001). Language-learning strategies: theory and perception. *ELT Journal,* Vol. 55/3, pp. 246-254.

Gulbahar, H. Beckett and Tammy Slater. (2005). The Project Framework: a tool for language, content, and skills integration. *ELT Journal,* Vol. 59/2, pp. 108-116. Oxford University Press.

Hamilton, Ruth. (2003). Spelling Strategy Teaching students to spell. *Modern English Teacher,* Vol. 12, No. 1, pp. 38-43.

Hargreaves, A. (1994). *Changing teacher's, changing times: Teachers' work and culture in the post-modern age***.** London: Cassell.

Harmer, Jeremy. (2001). *The practice of English language teaching*. Cambridge. Longman.

Harris, Barry.(2000). A Strategy for Identifying the professional Development Needs of Teachers: a report from New South Wales. *Journal of In-Service Education.* Vol. 26, No. 1, pp. 25-47.

Harste, C Jerome. and Kathy G. Short.(1996). Ken and Yetta Goodman: Exploring the roots of whole language. *Language Arts,* Vol. 73, pp. 508-519.

Hartas, Dimitra. (2005). *Language and communication difficulties*. Continuum, London New York.

Hayashi, Keiko. 1999. Reading Strategies and Extensive Reading in EFL classes. *Regional Language Centre,* Vol. 30, No. 2, pp. 114-116.

Hayes, David. (2000). Cascade training and teachers' professional development. *ELT Journal,* Vol. 54/2, pp. 135-145.

Haynes, Judie.(2007). Teaching Comprehension through conventions of Nonfiction Text. *Essential Teacher.* Vol. 2, Issue. 2, pp. 6-7.

Hopkins, Andy (1993).Teacher training and development. *MET Journal.* Vol. 2, No. 2.

Howarth, Patrick. (2002). Teachers and stress 1 What causes teachers to become stressed? *Modern English Teaching.* Vol. 11, No. 2, pp. 54-59.

Hsu, Shihkuan.(2005). Help-seeking behavior of student teachers. *Educational Research.* Vol. 47, No. 3, pp. 307-317.

Husu, Jukka. (2003). Real- world pedagogical ethics: mission impossible? *Teacher development,* Vol. 7, No. 2, pp. 311-327.

Hydkeby, S. and F. Breet. (1988). 'Using methodology note books on in-service teacher training courses.' *ELT Journal, 42/1.*

Inguva, M. (1995). 'Using Diaries for Teacher development'. Paper presented in All India seminars on teacher development at the regional institute of English, Bangalore**.** *input hypothesis. The modern language Journal. 73/4.440-464 Issues and innovations*. New Delhi: Sage publications.

James, A. Mark.(2006). Teaching for transfer in ELT. *English language teaching,* Vol. 60, No. 2, pp. 151- 201.

James, P. (2002). Teachers in Action: Tasks for in-service language teacher education and development. *ELT Journal,* Vol. 56, No. 2, pp. 203-20.

Jarvis, P. (1992). 'Using Diaries for teacher reflection on in- service courses' in hedge and Whitney (eds) *power pedagogy and practice,* OUP: 1996.

Jay, J. K., & Johnson, K. L. (2002). Capturing complexity: A typology of reflective practice for teacher education. *Teaching and teacher education, 18*(1), 73-85.

Jeannot, Mary. (2004). Investigating missed opportunities and cultural displays a reader reacts to Anne Lazaraton's "incidental displays of cultural knowledge in the nonnative- English-speaking teacher's classroom". *Tesol Quarterly Journal* Vol. 38, No. 2, pp. 325-33.

Jie, Li (2006). Language learning style and learning strategies of tertiary –level English learners in china. *Regional Language centre Journal,* Vol. 137, No. 1, pp. 67-89.

Johnson, David. (2000). Tips from the classroom. The cultural savvy minute: integrating culture, technology, and writing in an ESL composition class. *TESOL Journal.*

Johnson, K. E. (1992). The relationship between teachers' beliefs and practices during literacy instruction for non-native speakers of English. *Journal of reading behavior, 24*(1), 83-108.

Kapruan, Nardev. (1971). In-Service Education of Teachers on the USSR. *Teaching A quarterly Technical journal for teachers,* Vol. XLIII, No. 4, pp. 122-124.

Kebir, Catherine. (1994). An Action Research Look At The Communication Strategies of Adult Learners. *TESOL Journal,* Vol. 4, No. 1, pp. 28-31.

Kennedy, C. (1987). Innovating for change: Teacher development and innovation. *ELT Journal 41/3: 171-178.*

Kenny, Brian & William Savage. (1997). Language & Development: teachers in a changing world. *Asian Journal of English Language Teaching,* Vol. 7, pp. 121.

Khayum, Saleha. (2003). Tasks For Empowerment In English Language and Learning. *The English Classroom Bi- annual Journal,* Vol. 5, No. 1&2, pp. 140-163.

Khosla, D.N. (2001). Curriculum Framework for Quality teacher education. *ELT news.* Vol. 2, No. 1, pp. 20-24.

Kincheloe, J. L. (2012). *Teachers as researchers (classic edition): Qualitative inquiry as a path to empowerment.* Routledge.

Koprowski, Mark (2004). Strategies of Communication. *Modern English Teacher,* Vol. 13, No. 2, pp. 5-15.

Krashan, S. (1989).We acquire vocabulary and spelling by reading: Additional evidence for the Krishna and Lalitha Krishna. N. 2003. *Teaching English Approaches, methods, and techniques.* Chennai. Macmillan.

Kuc, Lidia. (1999). Do you know what your students want, what they really want? *Modern English teacher,* Vol. 8, No. 2, pp. 55-57.

Kumar, Sunil (1989). *"Promoting professional development of teachers of English: towards a holistic approach to INSET.*" Unpublished Ph. D Thesis. Hyderabad: CIEFL.

Kumar, Sunil (1991). Teacher development: A new concept. University news, May, pp. 1-2, *Taiwan. Teacher Development,* Vol. 2, No. 1, pp. 5-15.

Kumaravadivelu. B. (2003). Beyond Methods: Macrostrategies for Language Teachers. *ELT Journal,* pp. 339. *Reviews.*

Lalitha, C. (1994). *Diary study. In Teacher as researcher.* Hyderabad: CIEFL, pp. 8-9.

Lambert, Gray, Centra, et al. (1976). *A Guide for Evaluating Teaching for Promotion and Tenure*. New York: Center for Instructional Development, Syracuse University.

Larsen Freeman, Diane.(1978). An ESL index of development. *Tesol Quarterly. Vol. 12. No. 4. pp. 439-448.*

Larsen-Freeman, D. (1983). Training teachers or educating a teacher. *Georgetown University Round Table on Languages and Linguistics*, 264-274.

Larsen-Freeman, D. (2000). *Techniques and principles in language teaching.* Oxford: OUP.

Leo, Bartlett. (1990). '*Teacher development through reflective teaching. 'In Second language Teacher education*. Edited by jack, C. Richards and David Nunan. Cambridge: CUP.

Levin, B. Barbara.(2003**).** *Case studies of teacher development: An In- depth look at how thinking about pedagogy develops over time*. London. Lawrence Erlbaum associates.

Lindstromberg, Seth. 1997**.** *The Standby Book Activities for the language classroom*. Cambridge. Cambridge University Press.

Loughran, John and Deborah Corrigan (1995). Teaching portfolios: A strategy for developing learning and Teaching in pre-service education. *Teacher & Teacher Education,* Vol. 11, No. 6, pp. 565-577.

Lucas, Tamara and Suzanne Wagner. (1999). Facilitating secondary English language learners Transition into the mainstream. *ELT Journal,* Vol. 8, No. 4, pp. 6-12.

Macaro, Ernesto. (2003). Learning strategies in foreign and second language classrooms. *The English Teacher,* Vol. 6, No. 3, pp. 386-388.

Macleod, Flora & Michael Golby. (2003). Theories of learning and pedagogy: issues for teacher development. *Teacher development,* Vol. 7, No. 3, pp. 345-361.

Mann, Steve. (2005). The language teacher‘s development**.** *Language teaching,* Vol. 38, No. 4, pp. 103-118.

Marks, B. Merle and Particia Heffernan-Cabrera. 1977. Teachers' Attitudes towards Minority Group students – Is Pygmalion turning the tables? *TESOL Quarterly* Vol. 11.

Martin, A. Michel Sarah H. Martin,. And wang ying. (2002). The vocabulary self-Collection Strategy in the ESL Classroom. *Tesol Journal,* Vol. 11, No. 2, pp. 34-35.

Martiviano, M- Delmar & Vincente orquin. (1981). Identifying our students' strategies for learning English as a foreign language. *Modern English Teaching,* Vol. 9, pp. 38-41.

Mathew, R. (1998). *Grammar in communication Tasks for teacher development.* Hyderabad. Central Institute of English & Foreign language.

Mathew, R. (1998). *Just Write Tasks for teacher development*. Central Institute of English & Foreign languages, Hyderabad.

Mathew, R. (1998). *The Learner centered classroom Tasks for teacher development*. Central Institute of English & Foreign language, Hyderabad.

Mathew, R. (2013). 'Dairy writing as a tool for reflective practice' in R. Bolitho and A. Padwad (Eds), *Contunue Professional Development: Lessons from India.* New Delhi: British Council.

Mathew, R. (2015). 'Teacher development as the future of teacher education' in Pickering and Gunashekar (Eds), *Innovation in English Language Teacher Education*. New Delhi: British Council.

Mc Donough, H. Steven. (1995). *Strategy and skill in learning a foreign language.* London Edward Arnold.

Mc Ewan, K. Elaine. 2004. 7 *Strategies of Highly Effective Readers Using Cognitive Research to Boost K-8 Achievement.* California: Sage publications.

Mc Laughlin, M.W. and Talbert, J.E. (1990). 'The contexts in question: The secondary school workplace,' in M. McLaughlin, Talbert and n. Bascia. (eds)(1990) *The context of teaching in secondary schools: teachers' realities*. New York, Teachers College Press.

McDonough, Jo. (2002). The teacher as language learner: worlds of difference? *ELT Journal,* Vol. 56, No. 4, pp. 404-411.

McDonough, J. and McDonough, S. (1997). *Research methods for English language teachers*. London: Arnold Michael.

McGrath, J. E., & Kelly, J. R. (1986). *Time and human interaction: Toward a social psychology of time.* Guilford Press.

Mckay, Sandra Lee. (2000). Teaching English as an international language: implications for cultural materials in the classroom. *Tesol journal,* pp. 7-11.

McKay, S. L. (2006). *Researching second language classrooms.* Routledge.

McPhee, Alastair D. & Walter M. Humes. (1998). *Teacher education and teacher development: A Comparative Study. Teacher Development Journal,* Vol. 2, No. 2, pp. 165-178.

Mercer, Arah (2005). Vocabulary Strategy Work for Advanced Learners of English. *English Teaching Forum,* Vol. 43, No. 2, pp. 24-36.

Merideth, M Eunice. (2007). Leadership Strategies for Teachers. California: Evaluation. CIEFL, Hyderabad.

Merriam, S. B. (1998). "*Qualitative Research and Case Study Applications in Education. Revised and Expanded from Case Study Research in Education.*" Jossey-Bass Publishers, 350 Sansome St, San Francisco, CA 94104.

Merryfield, M Merry. (1993). Reflective practice in Global Education: Strategies for Teacher educators. *Theory into practice.* Vol. 32, No. 1. *Teacher Education in Global Perspectives (Winter, 1993).* pp. 27-32.

Mildred, G. McClosky. (eds) (1971). *Teaching Strategies and Classroom Realities.* New Jersey: Prentice – Hall.

Mistar, Junaidi. (2001). English learning strategies of Indonesian university students across individual differences. *Asian Journal of English language teaching,* Vol. 11, pp. 19-43.

Mochizuki, Akihiko.(1999). *Language learning strategies used by Japanese University students. RELC Journal,* Vol. 30, No. 2. pp.

Mohamed Naashia. (2006). Meaningful professional development. *English teaching professional. Issue 42, January 2006.*

Mohanraj, Jayashree. (1994). Developing Listening comprehension using easily available resources. *English teaching forum,* Vol. 32, No. 4, pp. 40-41.

Monippally, M. Mutthukutty. (2001). *Business communication strategies*. New Delhi, McGraw.

Moore, John and Neil Morrison (1988). *Some one Else's Problem? Teacher Development To Meet Special Educational Needs.* London: The Falmer Press.

Muijs, Daniel and David Reynolds.(2002).Teachers' Beliefs and Behaviors: What Really Matters? *Journal of Classroom Interaction,* Vol. 37, No. 2, pp. 3-13.

Mukherjee, H.B. (1960). Some Reflections on 'Teacher education'. *Teacher education* Vol. IV, No. 4, pp. 40-45.

Murdeswar, Meena (1998). *Evaluating teachers 'Guides: do teachers' Guides Guide teachers*?" Unpublished M.phil. Dissertation. Hyderabad: CIEFL.

Nagarajan. S. (1981). The decline of English in India: some historical notes. *College English Journal,* Vol. 43, No. 7, pp. 663-670.

Nakatani, Yasuo. (2005). The effects of awareness- Raising training on oral communication strategy use. *The modern language Journal,* Vol. 89, No. 1, pp. 76-91.

Narasimhaih, C. D.(1991), *N for Nobody: Autobiography of an English teacher.* New Delhi: B.R. Publishing Corporation.

National Curriculum Framework (2005) *NCERT,* New Delhi.

NCTE (1998), *Curriculum Framework for Teacher Education*. New Delhi.

NCTE (1998), *Curriculum Framework for Teacher Education: towards Preparing Professional and Humane Teacher*. New Delhi.

Newman, M Judith and Susan M. Church. (1990). Myths of whole language. *The Reading Teacher,* Vol. 44, No. 1, pp. 20-27.

Nunan, David. (2005). Styles and strategies in the language classroom. *The Language Teacher,* Vol. 29, No. 6, pp. 9-11.

Nunan, David. (2005). *Styles and strategies in the language classroom. The Language Teacher.* Vol. 29, No. 4, pp. 9-11.

Nunan, David.(1997). Strategy Training in the language classroom: an empirical investigation. *RELC Journal,* Vol. 28, No. 2, pp. 56-59.

Nunan, D. and C. Lamb. (1996). *The self directed teacher.* New York: Cambridge University Press.

Nunan, David (1986). Research Methods In Language Learning. Cambridge: Cambridge University Press.

Nunan. (1989). 'A client centered approach to teacher development.' *ELT Journal 43/2,* Oxford University Press.

O' Sullivan, C. Margo. (2002). Effective follow-up strategies for professional development for primary teachers in Namibia. *Teacher Development,* Vol. 6, No. 2, pp. 181-203.

Okita, Yoshio.(1996). Managing In- service Training. A Japanese Case study. *English teaching Forum,* Vol. 34, No. 2, pp. 18-21. 27-31.

Ortmeier, M.Christina. 2000. Project homeland: Crossing cultural boundaries in the ESL classroom. *Tesol Journal,* Vol. No. pp. 10-17.

Oxford, L.Rebecca. 1990. *Language learning strategies*. The University of Albama. Heinle & Heinle publishers.

Oxford, R. (1990). *Language learning strategies*. New York, 3.

Padwad Amol and Krishna Dixit (2014). *Continuing Professional development policy 'Think Tank'*: an Innovative Experiment in India.

Padwad, A. and Dixit, K. (2011). *Continuing Professional Development: An Annotated Bibliography*. New Delhi: British Council.

Panchal, Priyamvada. (2004). Teacher development: Mentorship. *ELT news,* Vol. 3, No. 3, pp. 44-46.

Panchal, Priyamvada. (2005). Life skills. *ELT News,* Vol. 4, No. 2, pp. 25-28.

Parrott, Martin (2000). *Grammar for English Language Teachers – With exercise and key*. Cambridge: Cambridge University Press.

Pollard, Andrew and Jill Bourne. (1994). *Teaching and learning in the primary school*. London and New York. Routledge Falmer.

Poongodi, O. T. (2003). Teaching Learning Strategies. *The English Classroom Bi-annual Journal,* Vol. 5, No. 1&2, pp. 113-139.

Prabhat S.V. (2002). Training of English Teachers. *ELT News,* Vol. 2, No. 3&4, pp. 8-16.

Prabhat. S.V. (2002). Training of English Teachers. *ELT News,* Vol. 1:2, No. 3&4, pp. 8-16.

Prabhu, N. S. (1987). *Second language pedagogy* (Vol. 20). Oxford: Oxford University Press.

Prabhu, N.S. (1990). There's no Best method, Why? *TESOL Quarterly, 24/2:*161-176.

Prabhu, N.S.(1991). *Second Language Pedagogy*. Oxford: Oxford University Press.

Quiring, Dean (2003). They are just students to me": strategies for addressing cultural differences in the school setting. Tesol Journal, Vol. 12, No. 2, pp. 3-4.

Razdan, Prithvi Nath.(1965). In-Service training of English teachers. Educational Review 71:7, pp. 153-56.

Regional Institute of English south. (2005). *Action research for development: An Anthology*. Bangalore. R.I.E. South India.

Regional institute of English, South India. (1985). *Impact of ELT training in southern Indian:* A RIESI study. Bangalore.

Reichelt, Melinda. (2000). Case studies in L2 teacher education. *ELT Journal,* Vol. 54/4, pp. 346-353.

Richard Watson Todd. 1999. Beyond Training. *Asian Journal of English language teaching,* Vol. 9, pp. 122-124.

Richard, J. C. and C. Lockhart. (1986). *Approaches and Methods in Language Teaching*. Cambridge: Cambridge University Press.

Richard, J. C. and C. Lockhart. (1996). *Reflective Teaching in Second Language Classrooms,* Cambridge: Cambridge University Press.

Richard, J. C. and C. Lockhart. (2001). *Approaches and Methods in Language Teaching. (2nd edition)*. New Delhi: Cambridge University Press.

Richards, C Jack, Gack and David Nunan. (1990). *Second language teacher education.* Cambridge. Cambridge University Press.

Richards, J. C. (1998). *Beyond training: Perspectives on language teacher education.* Cambridge University Press.

Richards, J. C., & Nunan, D. (Eds.). (1990). *Second language teacher education.* Cambridge University Press.

Richards, J.C. and T. S. Rodgers, (2003). *Approaches and methods in Language Teaching – A description and analysis.* Cambridge: Cambridge University Press.

Richards, J.C. (1998). *Beyond Training: Perspectives on Language Teacher Education.* Cambridge: Cambridge University Press.

Richards, J. (1998). *'Beyond Training.* New York: Cambridge University Press.

Ridgeway Ton. (2000). *Listening strategies- I beg your pardon? ELT Journal,* Vol. 54⁄2, pp. 179-185.

Roy, Chanda. (1985). *"The preparation of college and University teachers of English in India."* Hyderabad: CIEFL.

Rubdy, Rani. (1992). Teacher- Self- Image and the Teacher's Expanded Role. *CIEFL Bulletin,* Vol. 4, No. 1&2, pp. 55- 71.

Sampoornam, T.R.(2003). Quality-Key to Teacher Development. *English Language Teaching,* Vol. XXXIX, No. 6, pp. 32-35.

Saraswathi, V. (1991). The British council summer school: training the trainers. *The Journal of English language teaching. 6:2,* pp. 54-58.

Saraswathi, V. 1990. In-service teacher training for tertiary level in Indian thought from summer institutes. *The Madras Review of English studies 2:1,* pp. 2-11.

Savage, William. (1999). Strategies in learning and using a second language. *Asian Journal of English language teaching,* Vol. 9, pp. 115-119.

Sayer, J., & Jones, N. (2018). *Teacher training and special educational needs,* Routledge.

Scattergood, Ellen & Urawa Akenohoshi Gakuen. (2003). Encouraging the use of strategies to improve communication in the EFL classroom. *The Language Teacher.* Vol. 27, No. 6, pp. 3-9.

Sen, J. (2002). Understanding Teachers' Professional Growth Through Their Articulation of Personal Practical Knowledge. Journal of Education for teaching. Vol. 28, No. 1, pp. 75-78.

Sharkey, Judy. (2004). Teacher-Researcher collaboration in TESOL. Defining the process of teacher-Researcher collaboration. *TESOL Quarterly Journal,* Vol. 38, No. 2, pp. 335-338.

Sharma, Rahul Kumar. (1992). Initiating Teacher Development through Supervision. *CIEFL Bulletin,* Vol. 4, No. 1&2, pp. 31-71.

Sharma, R.K. (1989). *Problems and Solutions of Teaching English.* New Delhi.

Sharma, Rahul. 1991. *The teacher as facilitator: A new role for the language teacher.* "Unpublished M.Litt. Dissertation. Hyderabad: CIEFL.

Shuja, Asif. 2001. The use of communication Technology in the teaching of English language in India. *English studies India a Journal of English & language,* Vol. IX, pp. 86-102.

Simmons, M. (1999). The effects of an overt constructivist approach to learning mathematics and its subsequent defects on classroom teaching. *Teacher development,* Vol. 3, No. 2.

Skehan, Peter. (1989). *Individual Differences in Second- Language Learning.* London. Edward Arnold.

Smith, Kim. (1998). School models of teacher development: two cases for reflection. *Teacher Development,* Vol. 2, No. 1, pp. 105-121.

Smith, K. Valerie. (1989). Achieving communicative competence: games to develop communication strategies. *Modern English Teacher,* Vol. 16, No. 3/4, pp. 25-28.

Smith, A Colin. (2002). Supporting teacher and school development: Learning and teaching policies, shared living theories and teacher- researcher partnerships. *Teacher Development,* Vol. 6, No. 2, pp. 157-179. Commonwealth Publishers.

Smolen, Lynn; Carole Newman Tracey Wathen and Dennis Lee.(1995). Developing Student Self- Assessment Strategies. *Tesol Journal,* Vol. 5, No. 1, pp. 22-25.

Song Mi- Jeong.(1998). Teaching reading strategies in an ongoing EFL university reading classroom. *Asian Journal of English Language Teaching,* Vol. 8, pp. 41.

Sreekanth. (2007). Educational evaluation at school level success & failures. *Journal of community guidance & Research,* Vol. 24, No. 1, pp. 94-103.

Stenhouse, Lawrence. (1984). 'The teacher as focus of research and development.' in David Stephens. C and Jean E. Brown. 2000. *A Handbook of content Literacy Strategies: 75 Practical Reading and Writing.* Norwood, MA: Christopher-Gordon Publishers. (TESOL review)

Sterling, L. Chester (1960). In-service training. The workshop method. *Teacher education,* Vol. IV, No. 4, pp. 29-35.

Stern, H.H. (1992). *Issues and Options in Language Teaching.* Oxford: Oxford University Press.

Stern, H.H. (1983). *Fundamental Concepts in Language Teaching.* Oxford: Oxford.

Stufflebeam, D. L. (1971). The use of experimental design in educational evaluation. *Journal of Educational Measurement, 8*(4), 267-274.

Sugeng, Bombang (1997). A Learning strategy profile of Indonesian elementary school students. *Regional Language Centre,* Vol. 28, No. 2, pp. 82-83.

Sujatha, Priyadarshni. (2003). Teacher Development group As Means for Teacher Empowerment. *The English Classroom Bi-annual Journal,* Vol. 5, No. 1&2, 103-113.

Swan, M. (1985). A critical look at the communicative approach (2). *ELT Journal, 39(2),* 76-87.

Szabo, Anna. (1992). Teacher development-Do it yourself. *Modern English teacher,* Vol. 1, No. 1-3, pp. 23-27.

Talbot. (1997). Testing An L2 Reading strategy programme. *Regional Language centre,* Vol. 28, No. 2, pp. 128- 129.

Taylor, P. Barry. (1975). *Adult language learning strategies and their pedagogical implications. Tesol Quarterly,* Vol. 9, No. 4, pp. 391-399.

Tognozzi, Elissa. (2001). *The need for Teacher Development in technology. Italica.* Vol. 78, No. 4, *Linguistics and Pedagogy (Winter, 2001).* pp. 486-498.

Tomlinson Brian and Hitomi Masuhara.(2004). *Developing Cultural Awareness.*

Tomlinson Brian and Hitomi Masuhara.(2004). Developing Cultural Awareness. Integrating culture into a language course. *Modern English Teacher,* Vol. 13, No. 1, pp. 5-11.

Tomlinson. B. 1998. *Materials Development in Language Teaching*. Cambridge:

Tosey, Paul & Gill Nicholls. (1999). Ofsted and Organisational Learning: the incidental value of the dunce's cap as a strategy for school improvement. *Teacher development,* Vol. 3, No. 1, pp. 5-17.

Trites, Latricia. (2002). A Handbook of content Literacy Strategies: 75 Practical Reading and Writing. Tesol Journal, Vol. 10, No. 5/2/3, pp. 44-45. (Review)

Troike, S. (1976). *Strategies for Instruction*. Foundations for Teaching English as a Second language. London Prentice Hall. 7, pp. 98-126.

Vandergrift, Larry. (1999). Facilitating second language listening comprehension: acquiring successful strategies. *ELT Journal,* Vol. 53/3, pp. 168-175.

Varaprasad, Chitra. (1997). *Some Classroom Strategies developing critical literacy awareness. English Teaching Forum,* Vol. 35, No. 3, pp. 24-28.

Veloo, V.P. (1979).Teaching of English in India: A problem in search of a solution. *Regional Institute of English,* Vol. 1, No. 3, pp. 75-79.

Vulliamy, Graham. (1998). Teacher Development in Primary Schools: some other lessons from Taiwan. *Teacher Development,* Vol. 2, No. 1, pp. 5-15.

Wadden Paul & Sean Mc Govern.(1998).Learning Strategies: the key to god language learning. *Modern English Teacher,* Vol. 16, No. 3/4, pp. 38-40.

Walker, Tileston Donna. (2004). *What Every Teacher Should Know About Effective Teaching Strategies.* California: Corwin Press.

Wallace, J. Michael. (1998). Action Research for Language Teachers. *Modern English Teaching,* Vol. 8, No. 3, pp. 88-89.

Wallace, M. J., & Bau, T. H. (1991). *Training foreign language teachers: A reflective approach*. Cambridge University Press.

Wallace, J. (1998). *Action Research for Language Teachers.* Cambridge: Cambridge.

Watkins, Peter. (2007). *Learning to teach English. A practical introduction new teachers.* London. Viva Books Private Limited.

Watts. Noel. (1993). Communication Enhancement Strategies: CES use by Second Language Learners in LI and L2 Performance. *CIEFL Bulletin,* Vol. 5, No. 1&2, pp. 49- 59.

Watts, R. Noel. (1986). Developing Aural Anticipation and prediction Strategies. *English Teaching Forum.* Vol. XXIV, No. 1, pp. 21-23 and 29.

Weir, C.J. (1990). Communicative Language Teaching. London: Prentice Hall. *Whole Language Catalog,* California: American School Publishers.

Widdowson, H. G. (1983). *Learning purpose and language use*. Oxford Univ Press.

Williams, Ruth. (2005). The Role of Academic Study in Teachers' Professional Development. *Journal of In-Service Education,* Vol. 31. No. 3. pp. 455-469.

Williams, M. and Burden, R. (1997). *Psychology for Language Teachers*. Cambridge.

Woodward, T. (1991). *Models and metaphors in language teacher training: Loop input and other strategies*. Cambridge University Press.

Wilson, Rosemary. (2000). Teacher development: an opportunity for cross-cultural co-operation. *ELT Journal,* Vol. 54/1. pp. 65-71.

Withrow, Jean. (2003). *Effective Writing. Writing skills for intermediate students of American English.* Cambridge. Cambridge University Press.

Woods, D. (1996). *Teacher Cognition in Language Teaching: Beliefs, Decision-Making and Classroom Practice.* Cambridge: Cambridge University Press.

Woodward, T. (1991). *Models and metaphors in language teacher training: Loop input and other strategies.* Cambridge University Press.

Woolfolk, E. Anita Barbara Rosoff, and Wayne K. Hoy. (1990). *Teachers' sense of efficacy and their beliefs about managing students. Teaching & teaching education,* Vol. 6, No. 2, pp. 137-148.

Yang, Daping & Jianqiang Wu. (1999). Some issues in the reform and development of teacher education and training in China. *Teacher development,* Vol. 3, No. 2, pp. 157-171.

Yashpal Committee (1993) *'Learning without Burden'. Govt of India,* New Delhi.

Yin, R. K. (2009). Case Study Research: Design and Methods, Essential guide to qualitative methods in organizational research. *Applied Social Research Methods Series, 219.*

Yongqi, Gu Peter. (1996). Robinhood in SLA: what has the learning strategy researcher taught US? *Asian Journal of English language teaching.* Vol. 6, pp. 1-29.

Zellermayer, Michal. (1990). Teachers' development towards the reflective teaching of writing: An action research. *Teaching & teacher education.* Vol. 6, No. 4, pp. 337-354.

Zucker, Carol. (1993). Using whole language with students who have language and learning disabilities. *The Reading Teacher.* Vol. 46, No. 8, pp. 660-670.

Index

S

T